CHILD VISITATION INTERFERENCE IN FAMILY LAW LITIGATION

CHILD VISITATION INTERFERENCE IN FAMILY LAW LITIGATION

The Handbook for Victims of
Custody and Access Disputes

IRA DANIEL TURKAT, PH.D.

Copyright 2002

Library of Congress Cataloging-in-Publication Data

Turkat, Ira Daniel.

ISBN 0-9669516-0-3

The information provided in this book is based upon actual cases.
Certain aspects of the presentation have been modified to protect the
identities of the individuals involved.

For Derek, Holly, and Justin

CONTENTS

VIII

A NOTE OF CAUTION

This book will introduce you to a terrible tragedy known as child visitation interference. As you move through the various Chapters, despicable acts of cruelty, injustice, and viciousness will be exposed.

At times, you may experience certain emotional reactions such as sadness, anger, and frustration. Some of you may feel perplexed, shocked, and even outraged.

I have tried to relate what this problem, child visitation interference, is all about. I have deliberately tried to keep the discussion straightforward and without additional fury. In various instances, I may have succeeded to the point of appearing too dispassionate; if true, please forgive me. In those episodes of writing in which my own emotional reaction may have inflamed the discussion, I apologize as well.

The topic is not the easiest.

SECTION ONE

INTRODUCTION TO VISITATION INTERFERENCE

This Section will introduce you to some basic information about child visitation interference.

Chapter 1 reviews several key terms that are used when discussing visitation interference problems.

Chapter 2 illustrates how child visitation interference has come to affect millions of individuals in our society.

=1=

VISITATION AND
VISITATION INTERFERENCE

You lie by the pool on a beautiful summer day, enjoying your little son splashing and giggling, waving his love to you.

You walk up your driveway after a long day at work, to the adoring hug and smile of your sweet little daughter.

You brush the soft strands of hair that lie across your sleeping child's forehead, enjoying the expression on that lovable, innocent face.

You wake up in the middle of the night desperately missing these kinds of experiences, anguished that they have been unjustly stripped away from you, and realizing, that they may never be experienced again.

Welcome to the world of a parent suffering from child visitation interference.

For many parents, child visitation interference is an ongoing nightmare. It hits from all corners. It may come without warning. It might not go away. It hurts.

Badly.

Very badly.

In this book, we will explore the many faces of child visitation interference.

In order to properly discuss this topic, we must first outline some of the terms we will be using throughout the many pages that follow. So, before we get into the "blood, flesh and guts" of child visitation interference, let's first get ourselves familiar with the basic terms we will be using.

BASIC TERMS

Every divorced parent knows the term visitation.

Parents who are not familiar with the ongoings of divorce, often are unaware of the terms used when discussing this topic.

When a divorce occurs, a family is divided into two separate households. If there are children involved, one parent typically assumes responsibility for them the majority of the time. This parent is known as the custodial or residential parent.

The other parent usually has less time permitted with the child. This parent is known as the *noncustodial* parent. Sometimes, the noncustodial parent is referred to as the *visiting* parent or *nonresidential* parent.

When the term "visitation" is discussed, it typically refers to the legal right between a child and nonresidential parent to see each other. However, I believe that the term holds significantly more meaning than that.

DEFINING VISITATION

For me, visitation refers to the ongoing relationship between a divorced parent and child. That relationship spans many areas.

The telephone.

The school.

The mail.

The medical record.

The girl scouts meeting.

The tennis tournament.

The amusement park.

And so on.

When parents divorce, the laws of most states assume that it is important and beneficial for the children to visit with the nonresidential parent as much as is reasonably possible. When parents cannot agree on how much visitation there should be, most states have guidelines to help Judges create reasonable visitation schedules. An example might be as follows:

The nonresidential parent may visit with the child:
a) Friday 6 p.m. until Sunday 6 p.m. every other weekend.
b) Wednesdays from 5 p.m. until 8 p.m.
c) Christmas vacation.
d) Two weeks during the summer.

Yet, in another divorce case, the visitation schedule might be quite different:

The child may reside with the noncustodial parent:
a) The first and third week of each month from Wednesday after school until Sunday.
b) Eight consecutive weeks during the summer.
c) Every other year on the child's birthday.

In another case, the visitation arrangements might differ still. The visitation schedule might be spelled out in a Court Order as follows:

The child will reside with the primary residential parent from the Friday preceding the first day of school each year until the last day of the school year; the remaining time will be spent in the custody of the nonresidential parent.

Regardless of the specific days and times of visitation that a Court may award to a noncustodial parent, there are other visitation issues as well.

Most Courts would prefer that the child speak with the nonresidential parent any time the child desires. Similarly, most Courts would prefer to see the noncustodial parent be as involved in the child's school life and extra-curricular activities as both the parent and child prefer.

Thus, when we talk about visitation, we are talking about many different things which all have one central theme. Simply put, it is this: the child and visiting parent should be as involved with each other and see each other as much as is reasonable and possible.

DEFINING VISITATION INTERFERENCE

Now that we know what is meant by the term "visitation," we can discuss what is meant by the term *visitation interference*.

Visitation interference occurs when a child or parent is denied his or her legal rights of access to each other.

This definition captures the many faces in which visitation interference can reveal itself.

When the child is not permitted to spend a Court Ordered overnight visit with the nonresidential parent, that is visitation interference.

When a noncustodial parent is prevented illegally from speaking to his or her child on the telephone, that is visitation interference.

When a child's letter to a nonresidential parent is ripped up and thrown away by the custodial parent, that is visitation interference.

When a child's report card is denied to a noncustodial parent, that is visitation interference.

Using this definition, the reader can see that the term "visitation interference" means something more that just denying a parent the right to physically visit with his or her child. This definition refers to *the denial of the opportunity for the child and visiting parent to continue their relationship without unnecessary obstacles.*

In coming Chapters, we will discuss in detail many of the methods used when a custodial parent attempts to deny visitation to a nonresidential parent.

Before moving on however, the reader should be aware that in this book, I refer to child visitation interference only in the context of such interference being unjust. In other words, the parent who is being denied access has done nothing to deserve it.

Unjustified child visitation interference is abusive to both parent and child.

The following pages detail what this abuse is all about.

=2===========

THE VICTIMS

How common is visitation interference?

The answer to this question is not so easy to provide.

Visitation interference has not been measured as systematically as something like the census of the United States. However, we have some estimates of the problem that are available.

I must tell you, these estimates are very disturbing.

The Children's Rights Council in Washington DC estimates that 6,600,000 children are denied access to their nonresidential parent.

This is an astounding figure.

I say this for several reasons.

First of all, if we multiply this figure by two parents for each child, then we immediately see that 13 million parents are involved.

Second, if we assume that there is at least one grandparent alive for each parent of the child involved (hence, two grandparents), we can add another 13 million adults to the problem. This gives us 26 million adults in the United States who may know child visitation interference from firsthand experience.

Unfortunately, we are not done here.

What about aunts, uncles, cousins, friends, and others who are also denied visitation with the child? If we figure three such individuals per child we now must add almost 20 million more people to the equation. Including the 6,600,000 children whose visitation is denied, we are now talking about over 50 million people.

In the United States today, there are more than 250 million people. Using these figures, it would appear that one out of every five Americans has been touched by the problem of child visitation interference.

THE TROUBLING STATISTICS

Fifty million people is a lot of people! However, the picture may be even more disturbing.

The estimate that we started with was 6,600,000 children who are denied overnight visitation with their nonresidential parent. Now, I do not know for sure, but I believe that this estimate by the Children's Rights Council only represents those children who are denied overnight visitation. If this is so, there are probably even more children who may have overnight visitation but are denied telephone access and other avenues by which to interact with their nonresidential parent; *50 million Americans may be an underestimate of the number of people affected by child visitation interference.*

THE DIVORCING FAMILIES

Each year in the United States, approximately 1 million new marriages occur. Similarly, each year there are approximately 1 million divorces. Overall statistics suggests that about half of all new marriages will end in divorce. Even more troubling is the fact that an even higher percentage of second marriages will end in divorce. The number of children coming from divorced homes appears to be growing each year.

With this in mind, the following two studies are important. First, in his 1985 book on divorce, Dr. Kenneth Kressel reviews research that shows up to 40 percent of mothers who had custody, admitted denying visitation to their ex-husband in order to punish him.

Seven years later in 1992, a study of 125 divorced fathers was published by Dr. Joyce Arditti in the *Journal of Divorce and Remarriage.* Dr. Arditti reported that 50 percent of the divorced fathers said that their visitation was interfered with by the mother of the children.

These findings are alarming.

If 40-50% of all families of divorce are engaging in visitation interference, we are facing a problem of epidemic proportions.

WHO ARE THE VICTIMS OF VISITATION INTERFERENCE?

Earlier we made an estimate that perhaps as many as 50 million people in the United States alone are affected by child visitation interference.

Who are these victims?

It is the daughter who yearns for her father's embrace.

It is the son who wishes to hear his mother's voice on the phone.

It is the dad whose letters to his son are mailed but never received.

It is the grandmother who cries for the years lost between herself and her grandchild.

It is the neighbor who no longer can enjoy a game of "tag" with the children next door, because their mother has forbidden them to talk to anyone who is on speaking terms with her former husband.

The estimate of 50 million Americans I made earlier did not take into account a whole range of other people who become involved in a child visitation dispute.

For every divorce, there is a Judge. For every legal fight there are attorneys. For every attorney, there are secretaries and legal assistants. For every legal document, there are Court clerks.

In many cases, particularly when a custody battle is in progress, there are Guardians who become involved. Teachers become involved. Accountants become involved. Friends, acquaintances, basketball coaches, karate instructors, religious school educators, and others become involved. When one ponders all of the individuals who are touched by the child visitation interference problem, the figure is staggering.

The emotional, psychological and financial costs of child visitation interference are enormous. The impact is felt throughout our society.

In this sense, we are all victims of child visitation interference.

SECTION TWO

BASIC METHODS OF VISITATION INTERFERENCE

Over the years, I have seen many cases of visitation interference. I must tell you, that the parent who intends to interfere with visitation may display a wide range of strategies in denying access to the child involved. In this Section, I will expose you to many of the "dirty tricks" utilized. It saddens me that there are so many of these to discuss.

When examining child visitation interference, it is important for the reader to realize that no two cases of visitation interference are exactly alike.

Visitation interference cases differ in the type of activities that may be involved. They also differ in the severity of the activities that may be involved. There are some cases where the visitation interference lasts for a short time period; there are other cases where the interference may last for 10 years or longer.

In either case, little hearts are aching.

If you have experienced a situation involving child visitation interference, you may recognize some of the destructive actions I will describe. Most likely, you will discover that other people have experienced some awfully painful situations involving child visitation interference that you fortunately, have not.

If you have not been exposed to the problems between divorced parents regarding visitation interference, prepare yourself for a rude awakening.

3

HOME VISITATION
INTERFERENCE

One of the first places where a nonresidential parent may be introduced to visitation interference occurs at the former marital home.

Over the years, I have been exposed to many different methods used by custodial parents intent on interfering with the other parent's access to the child at the home. Let me share some of these with you.

THE "UNANNOUNCED—NOT AT HOME" METHOD

Observe the following scenario.

A father has separated from his wife and comes to visit with his children for the first time. The wife has agreed for the father to visit with the children that afternoon at 5 p.m. He drives up to the marital home. He is nervous, worried, and anxious to see his children. He parks the car and walks up to the front door, for the first time as a nonresident of the home where his children reside. He rings the doorbell. His wife opens the door and asks him what he wants. Startled by her question, he reminds her that he is here to see his children, as they agreed upon this time earlier in the day. She says to him that the children are not at home and slams the door in his face.

This scene reveals the "unannounced—not at home" strategy of visitation interference. With this method, the nonresidential parent spends the time, energy, costs, and emotional effort to carry through with visitation. The residential parent fails to inform the visiting parent that the children will not be there until *after* the noncustodial parent has arrived.

This type of visitation interference serves many purposes from the custodial parent's point of view.

First, it keeps the children away from the other parent.

Second, it punishes the visiting parent.

Third, it helps to teach the children that either the noncustodial parent didn't care enough to see them or that other activities are more important than seeing the noncustodial parent.

THE "NOT HERE—DON'T COME" APPROACH

A second method used to deny visitation at the home is the "not here — don't come" approach.

A custodial parent calls the visiting parent shortly before the visiting parent will come to visit with the children. During the phone conversation, the residential parent informs the other parent not to bother coming because the children are not there. No reason is given; they're simply not at home.

Sometimes, a particularly spiteful custodial parent will wait until *after* he or she is sure that the nonresidential parent has left his or her home and then leave a message on the nonresidential parent's answering machine. When the nonresidential parent arrives, the custodial parent can "innocently" ask, "Didn't you get my message?"

THE "SMOKE SCREEN" TECHNIQUE

The "Smoke Screen" manuever provides another variation of interference with home visitation. In this procedure, the custodial parent creates a "scene" at the child's primary residence.

Tom arrives to visit with his children. Tonya comes outside, closes the door behind her, and engages her former husband in an argument. She then goes back into the house and slams the door behind her. Tom tries to persuade her to open the door, so that he can see his kids. Tonya ignores him. After numerous unsuccessful attempts to see his children, he leaves in total frustration.

Use of the "smoke screen" maneuver can prove to be particularly exasperating. It puts the noncustodial parent in a real bind.

In the example above, the nonresidential parent had no intention of arguing with his former wife; he merely wished to visit with his offspring. The "smoke screen" procedure provided a convenient way for the custodial parent to not only upset the visiting parent, but to deny him access to his most treasured asset: his children.

THE "CHANGED LOCATIONS" METHOD

Divorce can often cause a great deal of instability. Many parents are quite sensitive to this issue. When it is in their power to do so, many parents will take extra care to try to reduce some of the instability for their children.

A simple way to help achieve this, is to strictly follow the visitation schedule. This shows commitment, responsibility, and regularity. The message given to the child is this:

> Even though I don't live with you anymore, I am still your parent and you can always count on me to be here for you.

The "changed locations" method is a visitation interference technique that specifically interferes with the message stated above. A typical scenario is as follows.

> The nonresidential parent comes to the former marital home at the agreed upon time and place. She walks up to the front door and sees there is a note waiting for her. She reads the note to learn that her children are not at home. According to the note, the children are waiting for her with their father at the park. She drives over to the park and does not see them. She goes through the entire parking lot and cannot find his car. She gets out, walks around, but still cannot find them. After an hour of waiting, she returns to the former marital home. No one is there. She goes back to the park. No one is there.

After several episodes of driving between the home and the park, the visiting parent gives up and returns to her apartment.

Like the previously described technique, the "changed locations" method simultaneously frustrates the noncustodial parent while denying access to the children.

THE "SCHEDULE LIE" MANEUVER

One of the most difficult methods to combat is when the custodial parent lies about a scheduled visitation.

A visiting parent comes to the primary residential home of the children expecting to see them. Upon arrival, the residential parent acts surprised to see the former spouse. The visiting parent asks where the children are. The custodial parent wants to know why the visiting parent wants this information. When the nonresidential parent states that it is her turn for visitation, the custodial parent replies that there must have been a mistake and maintains that it is not the appropriate time and place for visitation.

Individuals who lie about visitation arrangements in this way are particularly problematic to deal with. Often, the lying is not restricted to one episode. When one is forced to deal with a lying ex-spouse, it can make the visitation process a living nightmare.

THE "UPSET CHILD" ROUTINE

Divorcing parents often feel extra-sensitive about their children's well-being. Many parents feel a great deal of guilt about breaking up the family. Many feel that they have damaged their children by getting divorced.

The last thing a noncustodial parent wishes to do is to cause additional grief for one's offspring, especially if such grief is unnecessary. With this in mind, let us review an emotionally charged method of home visitation interference: the custodial parent's use of the "upset child" routine.

Roberta, a noncustodial parent, arrives at the designated time for visitation with her son. Her former husband, Marvin, emerges from the home and informs Roberta that their son is, "too upset to see you." Marvin goes back inside and closes the door. Worried and hurt, Roberta leaves without seeing her boy.

Sometimes, parents who use this procedure like to "dress it up" to improve its "punch".

"Nancy doesn't want to see you."

Or perhaps:

"John is too angry with you to spend any time with you today."

By "dressing up" the technique in this way, the nonresidential parent is specifically blamed for the negative emotions the child is purported to be experiencing.

In this situation, the visiting parent basically has no recourse. The child is "locked away" inside. The custodial parent denies access to the home.

The noncustodial parent is forced to leave with the thought that the child is "upset" with the visiting parent.

THE "OTHER ACTIVITY" METHOD

Another procedure utilized for home visitation interference is the "other activity method." Here, the noncustodial parent arrives only to learn that the child is off at some other event or activity.

The nonresidential parent may be told something like this:

"Johnny went to Mary's birthday party"

Other variations might include:

"There is a big test tomorrow so David is studying at Bill's house"

"Crissy is at gymnastics class ... it's the only time that she could get in."

A more spiteful approach is to arrange for the child to have unusually rewarding activities at other locations, when visitation is typically scheduled.

For example, the custodial parent can make arrangements for the child to go to an amusement park with one of the child's friends. When the noncustodial parent arrives, she learns that not only will the child not be there for her to see, but the child is out having a great time.

In this way, the visiting parent not only misses seeing the child, but also may experience feelings of rejection and loneliness.

THE "RUNNING LATE" MANEUVER

Many visiting parents are super-conscious of time issues when it comes to visitation periods. With restricted access to the children, time is a precious commodity.

Every minute seems to count.

For noncustodial parents who feel this sense of time appreciation, the "running late" maneuver provides another frustrating source of home visitation interference.

Here, visitation which is scheduled, for example, at 5 p.m., is manipulated by the residential parent so that it doesn't occur until 5:40 p.m. However, because scheduled visitation ends at 7:30 p.m., the noncustodial parent loses the time with the child.

It should be noted that in some Court specified visitation guidelines, there is a "grace period" included; typically, 45 minutes. In other words, in transferring the children one is obligated to wait 45 minutes for the other parent. This gives significant leeway for the spiteful parent in reducing the visiting time.

Should the parent who has lost the 45 minutes of visitation time just add it on to the end of the scheduled visitation period? Unfortunately, doing so generates its own set of problems.

We will address this issue later on in Section Four and also in Section Eight.

THE "MULTIPLE SCHEDULE" TACTIC

When multiple children are involved in the divorce, the room for additional visitation interference grows.

For example, in a situation where the noncustodial parent is supposed to pick up the children at the primary residence at a particular time, the custodial parent could manipulate the various children's schedules to make it very difficult for the visiting parent.

A father of three children was to visit with them on a weekday afternoon from 4 p.m. until 7 p.m. The mother loaded the children's schedule with extra-curricular activities so that the father would have to pick up one child at one place at 4 p.m., a second child who was located a 30 minute drive away at 4:45 p.m., and the last child to be picked up back at the primary residence at 5:15 p.m.

In this example of the "multiple schedule" technique, the majority of the "visitation time" was spent in the car, as opposed to high quality time that could have been spent between the children and their visiting parent. Furthermore, because two children's extra-curricular activities were scheduled during parts of the visitation period, this time with the nonresidential parent was lost as well.

THE "INCOMPATIBLE SCHEDULE" TECHNIQUE

A more spiteful variation of the "multiple schedule" technique is to schedule the children's activities at different locations for the *same* time. In this way, the nonresidential parent cannot possibly be with all the children simultaneously.

This technique provides a no-win scenario for the noncustodial parent. The choices are to:

1. Lose time with at least one of the children;
2. Prevent at least one of the children from going to his or her scheduled activity;
3. Keep all of the children together and not attend any of their scheduled activities.

The reader can plainly see that somebody loses no matter which option is chosen.

At this point you have undoubtedly noticed that there are many mean and rotten ways for a bitter custodial parent to both deny visitation and torment the ex-spouse simultaneously. You may also feel that all of this is terribly wrong, misguided, and even abusive.

It is.

Unfortunately, these types of incidents are occuring and re-occuring all across this country, every single day.

4

TELEPHONE VISITATION INTERFERENCE

One of the greatest conveniences of modern life is the ability to speak on the telephone with someone who is a significant distance away. In divorce situations involving children, the knowledge that one's parent is only a phone call away can be very reassuring to a child.

It can also be very reassuring to a parent.

In the best case scenario, noncustodial parents speak on the phone with their children several times a week. Children are able to freely relate their day to day experiences and receive the enthusiastic encouragement that only a parent can provide. Anytime the parent or child feels an urge to speak with the other, the telephone enables a sharing of their life together.

Unfortunately, certain parents find the telephone to be an excellent avenue for interrupting visitation between the child and nonresidential parent.

Let's review some of the techniques utilized.

THE "HURRY UP" TECHNIQUE

The first procedure to be described is what I refer to as the "hurry up" technique.

A nonresidential parent and child are on the telephone. A few minutes into the conversation, the custodial parent informs the child that the phone needs to be used and therefore, the conversation must end.

Repeated use of this strategy insures that the child and visiting parent will have minimal access to each other by phone. Further, after repeated experiences like this, both the parent and child begin to feel frustrated. In this way, telephone calls from the noncustodial parent begin to take on a negative quality, even though the nonresidential parent has done nothing wrong.

From the perspective of the manipulative interfering parent, an additional advantage accrues by using this procedure: he or she can "honestly" claim that the child talks to the nonresidential parent whenever that parent calls.

THE "EXCUSE" MANEUVER

A second procedure utilized by various residential parents to interrupt telephone visitation with their child is to use the "excuse" method.

> A father calls to speak with his son. He is told that the child is eating dinner and to call back later. The father follows his ex-wife's instructions and calls back later. Now he is told that the child is doing his homework. He is told once more to call back later. When the father calls back for a third time, he is told that the child was tired and went to bed early.

On the face of it, the above "excuses" seem viable. However, after repeated experiences like this, the father comes to realize that there is a deliberate interference with his telephone access to the child.

The types of excuses offered can be quite varied.

"She is playing now"
"She is in the shower now"
"She is watching TV"
"She is in the back yard"
"She just stepped outside with a friend"

After a while, it appears that there is *never* a good time to call.

THE "HANG UP" PROCEDURE

A less subtle method for telephone visitation interference is the "hang up" technique. It's lack of subtlety however, does not weaken it's effectiveness.

In this procedure, whenever the custodial parent receives a phone call from the noncustodial parent in which there is a request to speak to the child, the custodial parent merely hangs up the phone.

After several episodes of being unable to get past the "hang up," the visiting parent quickly gets the message that attempts to speak with the child on the phone will be unsuccessful.

In time, the noncustodial parent may conclude that it is a waste of time to even try calling the child; so the calls are no longer attempted. Unfortunately, the child may begin to feel rejected because it appears that the visiting parent is no longer calling.

THE "NO MESSAGE" PLOY

Related to the "hang up procedure" is a "teasing" strategy, which I refer to as the "no message" ploy.

In this particular approach, whenever the nonresidential parent calls and asks to speak to the child, the residential parent indicates that the child is not available but reassures the caller that he or she would be happy to take a message. After taking the "message", the residential parent makes sure *not* to give the "message."

Using this procedure, the child has no idea that the noncustodial parent has called. Likewise, the nonresidential parent is unclear as to why the child has not called back.

Both may feel rejected.

THE "STAND BY" TECHNIQUE

A powerful way to disrupt telephone visitation is to utilize the "stand by" procedure.

In this method, the child is allowed to speak to the nonresidential parent but the custodial parent stands next to the child during the phone conversation. The custodial parent may accentuate his or her feelings of disapproval by keeping hands crossed against the chest, tapping a foot, looking angry, and so on. Within a short period of time, the child learns that the custodial parent does not want the child to be talking with the nonresidential parent.

If this is done continuously, the interfering parent may eventually coerce the *child* to terminate the telephone visitation without the custodial parent having to say anything. When this is accomplished, the nonresidential parent (unaware of the pressure placed on the child by the custodial parent) may feel rejected *by the child.*

Often, the child does not feel too good either about what he or she has been coerced to do.

THE "HOLD ON" MANEUVER

An exasperating method of telephone visitation interference occurs when the custodial parent engages in the "hold on" procedure.

In this method, whenever the nonresidential parent calls, the custodial parent gets on the telephone and tells the nonresidential parent something like this:

"I'll be happy to put Amanda on, let me put you on hold."

The nonresidential parent is then put on hold and Amanda is never told that the parent is waiting to speak with her.

In this way, the nonresidential parent ends up on hold until he or she hangs up in frustration. Indeed, a very long period of time may elapse.

THE "AVERSIVE CONVERSATION" TECHNIQUE

The "aversive conversation" technique is a powerful telephone visitation interference strategy, used by a select group of custodial parents.

In this procedure, whenever the nonresidential parent calls, the custodial parent harrasses the caller by screaming at, yelling at, cursing at, and/ or trying to argue with the caller. This behavior by the custodial parent puts the nonresidential parent in a difficult dilemma.

If a call is placed to the child, a barrage of punishment is guaranteed. If no call is made, there will be no contact with the child.

Unfortunately, in many cases where the "aversive conversation" technique is employed, the punishment is so painful to the nonresidential parent, that calls are no longer made.

As the reader can see, what could be a significant source of comfort for a child of divorce and a noncustodial parent, the telephone, can be spitefully manipulated by a self-serving residential parent.

=5=

MAIL VISITATION INTERFERENCE

I have yet to meet a child that does not like to receive mail.

Mail can be fun.

Mail can be exciting.

At times, a child who receives mail may feel as if he or she is getting a gift. Others feel "grown up" when they receive mail.

For whatever reason children enjoy receiving mail, it is an important medium by which a nonresidential parent and child can maintain their relationship.

In this section, I will outline four methods that are used for cutting off mail visitation.

THE "SCREENING" METHOD

The first interference procedure to be described is the "screening method." This procedure may be adapted to both mail incoming to the child and/or mail outgoing to the nonresidential parent.

In the "screening" procedure, the custodial parent literally checks the contents of the mail before it is given to the child or allowed to go out to the noncustodial parent.

The methods used vary from case to case.

In certain cases, a residential parent might literally open incoming mail right in front of the child. In other cases, a more devious residential parent may steam open the envelope, read the contents, and then decide whether or not to let the mail move on to it's intended recipient.

THE "DELAY" METHOD

A second method utilized for mail visitation interference, is to use the "delay" maneuver. Observe the following example.

> It is Christopher's birthday. Christopher is expecting to receive many birthday cards in the mail. Christopher's father screens all of the incoming birthday cards until the one from the boy's mother is identified. Her card is secretly stored away. Six days after Christopher's birthday, the birthday card from his mother "arrives" in the mail.

Since the nonresidential parent's birthday card did not arrive on time (as far as Christopher is concerned), the child is obviously disappointed. In some cases, the child may feel more than disappointment.
Some may feel rejection.
Some may feel anger at the parent whose card did not arrive on time.
More on children's reactions in Section Five.

THE "DISCOURAGEMENT" TECHNIQUE

The third procedure used to disrupt mail visitation is to engage the "discouragement" technique. In this approach, the custodial parent basically encourages the child *not* to write a letter to the visiting parent.
The strategy used can vary considerably from case to case. For example, when a child states that he or she would like to write a letter to the noncustodial parent, the residential parent may something like, *"That's a good idea, but lets work on it later"*; "later" never seems to come.
Other variations of this approach include:

"I don't know if we have time now to write the letter"
"Let's talk about that later"
"Are you sure she will really want a letter from you?"
"He didn't write back the last time, so why bother?"

THE "CUT OFF" PROCEDURE

The last mail visitation interference technique I will describe is the "cut off" method.

Simply put, in this technique, contact by mail is literally terminated. When letters arrive from the former spouse, they are discarded before the child can learn about them. When the child writes letters and asks the custodial parent to mail them, reassurance is given that they will be mailed but the letters secretly end up in the trash.

Many noncustodial parents who have been denied mail visitation, often find themselves bewildered as to why they are not getting responses from their offspring. In some cases, it may take years before the clever manipulations of the interfering custodial parent are discovered.

In brief, the fun and excitement that mail seems to bring out in children, as well as the comfort it can provide a child coping with divorce, is transformed by a vicious custodial parent into a personal whipping tool.

=6=

SCHOOL VISITATION INTERFERENCE

To this point, we have seen many rotten manuevers that a parent dedicated to child visitation interference can pull off quite easily, in the convenience of one's home.

Unfortunately, such foul manipulation of children does not always stay in the home.

What's even worse, some families are exposed to actions even more vicious than what I've described already. As we move on, you'll see what I mean.

If at this point, you find yourself quite disturbed from learning how the home, the phone, and the mail are manipulated, you may want to take a break before we proceed into vicious activities outside of the home. For those ready to press on, let's talk about school.

School represents one of the major influences in a child's life. The good parent wants to be involved in his or her child's school life. A good teacher wants the parent to be involved as well.

School visitation can include a variety of activities and interfaces with the school system.

A parent may wish to have lunch with his or her child.

He or she may wish to sit in the child's classroom to observe the educational atmosphere and teaching skill of the instructor.

A parent may wish to participate in parent-teacher conferences.

In addition, there are often school plays, carnivals, and other special events in which parents and children can come together. Naturally, access to the child's school records is important. Finally, when other school services become necessary, such as social work evaluations, psychological assessments, standardized tests, and so on, the active parent desires involvement.

The type of visitation interference activities that are engaged in, basically fall into three general categories.

First, are the methods used *directly* by the custodial parent to the noncustodial parent. These include the "false information" and "black out" techniques.

Second, are the *indirect* methods in which the custodial parent interfaces with the school in a way designed to restrict visitation. These include the "sole contact" and "legal threat" manipulations.

Finally, there are *specific activities* at the school that the residential parent intent on visitation interference can engage in. These include the "promoting discomfort" technique and the "valued volunteer" strategy.

Below I will describe each of the procedures that are used in these categories.

THE "FALSE INFORMATION" MANEUVER

In the "false information" maneuver, the residential parent does just that: he or she transmits inaccurate information to the visiting parent.

Use of the "false information" technique may be used in a variety of ways.

First, the procedure may be applied to important dates (such as the day little Billy is required to take the annual state exam in order to be allowed to graduate from the second to the third grade).

Second, the maneuver can be used with important times (such as the school play that Billy is to be in).

Finally, the "false information" method can be utilized with special events (such as Billy's surprise birthday party).

Take the following example:

In the early stages of a bitter custody battle, a nonresidential father was eager to attend his son's first ever school team soccer practice. Although it was not a good time work-wise to do so, with a significant effort, the father was able to rearrange his schedule at work to be able to come to the soccer practice. He arrived at the field minutes before the time his divorcing wife said tryouts would begin. Unfortunately, no one was there. The information provided was wrong. Practice was already over.

In this example, not only did the father miss his son's soccer practice, he can *never* recapture attending his son's *first ever* practice again.

It's over.

He missed it.

Clearly, when a custodial parent uses the "false information" manuever, the nonresidential parent is usually left "holding the bag."

THE "BLACK OUT" TECHNIQUE

The second method of school visitation interference to be discussed is the "black out" method. Here, the custodial parent refuses to provide the nonresidential parent *any* information pertaining to the child's school.

Report cards are not sent.

Special events are not announced.

School schedules are thrown away.

The nonresidential parent who is unaware of his or her rights in the matter, will basically be devoid of opportunities and experiences to participate in school visitation.

In this way, the child and nonresidential parent are effectively "blacked out" from school visitation with each other.

THE "SOLE CONTACT" MANEUVER

The second category of school visitation interference involves the *indirect* methods. Two such procedures will be discussed. First, I will describe the "sole contact" technique.

In this procedure, the custodial parent makes certain that he or she is the *only* parent involved with the school.

Schools systems often assume that the only interactions with parents will be through the mother, and therefore deal directly and exclusively with her. In fact, many of the record forms used in certain school systems are designed to require the name, address, and phone number of only one parental household.

In school systems that leave room for separate information about both parents, the parent who purposely leaves off information about the other parent can often become the sole contact with little effort.

Some attempts to be the sole contact may be so outlandish as telling the school that the former marital partner is no longer living.

THE "LEGAL THREAT" PLOY

The second type of indirect procedure to be discussed is the "legal threat" ploy.

In this approach, the custodial parent specifically informs the school employee (be it the teacher, principal or office secretary) that legal action is pending or accomplished (with papers "to be drawn up") that will prevent the nonresidential parent from having any knowledge, information, or access to the child through the school.

The mere mention of such things by a custodial parent, often propels the school system into a strict defensive posture.

In the early stages of a hotly contested custody battle, one mother told a school secretary in the main office, that "papers were being drawn up" that would prevent the father from having any access to his children or information about them at their school. The mother's claim was totally false. Nevertheless, the school went into action. The children's teachers refused to speak with the father when he called. He was not allowed to have lunch with his children at school either. The father was forced to engage in costly legal action to restore his school visitation rights.

When the custodial parent makes claims of this kind and the claims are accepted as true, the school system feels required to "protect" the child. Generally, school systems are conservative in nature and are more likely to err on the side of "better to be safe than sorry."

In such situations, the noncustodial parent who does not persist in gaining access will be effectively prevented from interacting with his or her child at school, obtaining school records, and/or interacting with school personnel.

THE "PROMOTING DISCOMFORT" TECHNIQUE

The last category of school visitation interference to be addressed is the *specific activities* group of maneuvers. This category involves two distinct approaches. These include the "promoting discomfort" technique and the "valued volunteer" strategy.

I will first present the "promoting discomfort" technique.

In this approach, the custodial parent identifies the appropriate "target" and then creates a "scene" to effectively prevent the nonresidential parent from visiting with the child at school.

The "target" may vary depending on the case. Whereas one custodial parent may try to intimidate a teacher, another custodial parent may "target" the school's Principal.

When the child is the "target", the goal is to upset the child to the point that enough discomfort is generated to preclude the nonresidential parent from being accepted on the campus.

Some examples should help illustrate the power of this technique.

> One noncustodial father tried to visit with his daughter at school. The child's mother made her feel so guilty about talking with her father, that the little girl refused to see him when he came.

> A mother made such a fuss at a Principal's office that the Principal advised the father that he could not see his son on the school grounds.

In certain cases, the discomfort to be promoted may be aimed directly at the nonresidential parent when he or she attempts to visit with the child at school. Such interactions may cause the noncustodial parent sufficient discomfort to lead him or her to unilaterally withdraw from interacting at the school.

> One father went to have lunch with his child at school. His belligerent divorcing wife followed him there. Additionally, she brought her good friend who was verbally hostile to the child's father. In front of the child and other classmates, the two women cursed at him until he left.

THE "VALUED VOLUNTEER" STRATEGY

A powerful technique for school visitation interference is the "valued volunteer" strategy. Here, the custodial parent makes a significant commitment of time and effort to the school which the child attends.

Working as a volunteer, the school is appreciative of the free help that is provided. In return, the custodial parent is now positioned to wedge additional control over events pertaining to the child at school.

Observe the following example.

> A mother who was viewed as a helpful volunteer gained the ability to enter her daughter's classroom prior to her lunch period. Whenever the noncustodial parent came to have lunch with his daughter, the volunteer mother prevented it from occuring.

The reader should keep in mind that schools usually try to be as fair as possible in dealing with both custodial and nonresidential parents. However, school administrators are motivated to keep the school grounds as a "safe haven" for its children.

Rightly so.

School personnel are highly motivated to reduce the opportunities for combative parents to battle on school grounds. The last thing that a school Principal wants to encourage is a kidnapping of a child or, a shooting on the school premises.

When presented with two fighting parents, the "impartial" school administrator who is motivated to avoid conflict, will typically opt to support the parent known best: the volunteer.

By supporting the volunteer, the school administrator has avoided two potential problems. First, the volunteer provides hours of free help at the school. Should the volunteer parent not be supported, the volunteer may quit. Thus, the school would stand to lose the extra work it receives at no charge to its budget.

The second potential problem avoided is what an angry volunteer might do if not supported. He or she could stir up teachers, other school personnel, or other volunteer parents to be angry with the school administrator. Remember: *no school administrator wants additional problems on his or her campus.*

Thus, when the conflict between two fighting parents is brought to the school grounds, the volunteer is more likely to achieve what he or she is after.

As the various techniques of school visitation interference demonstrate, the school is merely a playground for the custodial parent who chooses to play these destructive games. With determination, the interfering custodial parent can literally shut out the noncustodial parent from participating in the educational experiences of one's children.

7

OUTSIDE ACTIVITY VISITATION INTERFERENCE

A primary opportunity for visitation interference involves the outside activities of the children involved.

These may include organized activities such as softball, soccer, gymnastics, girl scouts, music lessons, and the like. Ceremonies represent another area for visitation, including religious gatherings, graduations, birthday parties and other events.

The methods utilized for visitation interference in these areas include many of the procedures outlined in the preceding sections. For example, soccer participation involves scheduling for team games, team practices, team picnics, awards ceremonies, and other events. The use of the "false information" maneuver or the "black out" technique (see Chapter 6) are potent visitation interference strategies.

In addition to the above, I will introduce you to two additional techniques that are often used in these types of situations.

THE "BARRIER" TECHNIQUE

The first procedure to be described is the "barrier" technique. It basically goes like this:

At one of the events mentioned above, the custodial parent (either alone or with the aid of others) physically shields the child during any opportunity for potential interaction with the nonresidential parent. In other words, a "human barrier" is created for the noncustodial parent.

Any attempt by the nonresidential parent to interact with the child is physically thwarted by at least one person.

> A father came to see his son at a "Little League" baseball game. Whenever the father tried to get close enough to talk with his son, the custodial mother and her friend would immediately move in between them to prevent the father and son from interacting.

If the participants in the "barrier" have decided to be particularly hostile, the interchange can rapidly escalate already heated emotions into a serious public conflict.

Clearly, the "barrier" technique can prove to be an especially potent procedure.

THE "CHILD KNOWS" METHOD

Most children are highly motivated to please their parents. The desire for a parent's approval often is intensified during a divorce. Unfortunately, some divorcing parents will take advantage of this to disrupt the other parent's visitation. It puts the child in a terrible predicament.

In the "child knows" method, the custodial parent has repeatedly and intensely made it clear to the child that he or she is not to interact with the nonresidential parent. When this occurs, it can be particularly devastating to both child and visiting parent.

The child may avoid the visiting parent's gaze.

The child may ignore the noncustodial parent's words.

The child may act non-responsively to any actions by the visiting parent.

The pressure exerted by the interfering parent may be strong enough to cause a vibrant child to act like an emotionless looking robot.

It should be noted that the pain of such behavior may be intense for both child and nonresidential parent. However, the child may view acting in this way as being the lesser of two evils; a more potent punishment by the custodial parent may be awaiting the child, if the instructions are not properly carried out.

Although as horrid as this scenario might appear, things can in fact, get worse.

Often they do.

It is with this thought in mind that we move to the next Section which discusses the more extreme methods of visitation interference.

SECTION THREE

EXTREME METHODS OF VISITATION INTERFERENCE

This Section will describe some of the extreme methods utilized in a campaign of visitation interference.

Individuals who engage in these types of behavior, typically use many of the methods that I mentioned in earlier Chapters.

They manipulate the phone.

They deny visitation at the home.

They interfere at the child's school.

Clearly, use of these methods cause significant pain.

However, those who engage in the extreme methods of visitation interference, do much more. The pain and discomfort they provoke takes visitation interference to another level.

8

PARENTAL ALIENATION SYNDROME

Dr. Richard Gardner is a prominent psychiatrist who has published many books which discuss what he describes as the "Parental Alienation Syndrome." Unfortunately, there is virtually no research on the Parental Alienation Syndrome. However, Dr. Gardner reports his observations and theories from a wealth of experience in this area. Given the limited space in which I can present his ideas in this book, I highly recommend Dr. Gardner's writings be consulted by the reader interested in this topic.

THE DEFINITION

What precisely is Parental Alienation Syndrome? In a nutshell, a parental alienation exists when *a child is successfully taught to become obsessed with negative aspects of a parent that are unjustified.*

Let us break this definition down to its parts.

First, the child is *obsessed* with negative aspects of a parent. In other words, the child is preoccupied with these criticisms. The child who has occasional negative comments about a parent does not have Parental Alienation Syndrome.

A *second* part of the definition is that the negative aspects of a parent are *unjustified.* This typically presents itself in either of two forms. The child's allegations are either:

    1) untrue; or

    2) partially true but greatly exaggerated.

Let's examine an untrue claim.

A child may allege that one of the parents was physically abusive when in fact, that parent had *never* engaged in any abusive behavior. Nevertheless, the child maintains that the parent was abusive and makes the claim with intensity.

Now let's examine when the child becomes obsessed with a partially true but greatly exaggerated criticism of the parent.

A parent who has an occasional alcoholic drink may be referred to as a "drunk."

A parent who is in therapy for a relatively minor problem may be described as a "psycho" or "mental patient."

A parent who takes aspirin for headaches may be described as a "drug addict."

Whether partly true and exaggerated, or totally untrue, the child suffering from a Parental Alienation Syndrome remains obsessed with these criticisms which are basically unjustified.

An important aspect of the definition of a Parental Alienation Syndrome is that the parent who is teaching the child to be alienated and the child together are considered as having the syndrome. *Children are not born with this disorder.* They are taught to experience these things and it is both the teacher and the pupil who suffer with this syndrome.

THE ALIENATED PARENT

The reader who has never been exposed to an individual with a Parental Alienation Syndrome may be totally perplexed as to how such a thing could develop if the child had a loving relationship with the parent who is the target of the syndrome. The reader who ponders this issue should know that the parent who is the recipient of the Parental Alienation Syndrome often remains even more perplexed.

Imagine for the moment, that you are the parent of a child who is falsely making a claim that you sexually abused her. What would that feel like?

Think about it.

Truly try to imagine the feeling.

Now, take that feeling and multiply it by 100,000. This will give you some idea what a loving parent goes through when targeted by one's own child for development of a Parental Alienation Syndrome.

I have seen grown men cry their eyes out as they describe how their children have been taught to hate them. As the tears flow, they tell me how loving and wondrous their relationships with their children were before the divorce. They show me pictures of them with their children, arm in arm, hand in hand, love overflowing.

The pain of the alienation hovers about them.

HOW COMMON IS IT?

Gardner estimates that 90 percent of all custody battles will show some aspect of Parental Alienation Syndrome. It is important to note that Gardner does not mean that 90 percent of all custody battles cause a full-blown Parental Alienation Syndrome. Rather, he means that the nature of the custody battle seems to bring out at least some types of alienating behavior.

In his experience, Gardner estimates that 90 percent of the time it is the mother who is the alienator in the custody battle. In 10 percent of the cases, Gardner believes it is the father who creates the Parental Alienation Syndrome. In either case, let us focus briefly on the nature of the custody battle, so the reader can appreciate how a Parental Alienation Syndrome may come about.

THE CUSTODY BATTLE

Divorce is a difficult experience for most. Dissolving a relationship which has had strong emotional aspects is quite demanding. Ending the emotional ties are challenging enough, but now the couple's assets and liabilities must be split up as well. Possessions need to be divided.

Relationships with others change.

Changes of residence occur.

All of these experiences are stressful. But if there are children involved, the stresses multiply enormously.

Approximately 90 percent of children who live with a single parent live with their mother. Fathers rarely seek custody of their children. However, when the parents cannot agree as to who should be the primary residential parent, the stresses unfold even more.

The term "custody battle" correctly indicates the nature of legal proceedings over the custody of children in a divorce. That is, an adversarial process unfolds. However, it has been the author's experience that custody proceedings are more like warfare, composed of multiple and diverse battles. In some respects, I think the term, "custody war" would be more applicable.

Nevertheless, the term "custody battle" is the most widely used and thus, I will follow convention.

THE CUSTODY COMBATANTS

Who are the participants in a custody battle?

The two major "generals" are the husband and wife who are now divorcing. Typically, they have had a significant history of major disagreement about many things which has led to their divorce. Now they are disagreeing big time over their children. And they believe strongly that it is in their children's best interest that they live with them, as opposed to the other parent.

Individuals who engage in a custody battle must have at least two important assets. First, they must have a strong conviction. Second, they must have a significant source of money to pay for the legal proceedings.

To get an idea about the first requirement, one should think about two religious radicals who have opposing beliefs about the same thing. For example, imagine the militant Islamic fundamentalist and the ultra orthodox Jew who both believe in their hearts that God wants them to have total ownership of Jerusalem.

Both have the same consuming feeling of being on a mission from God.

Both are willing to endure as much pain and suffering as is necessary to win.

Both are willing to destroy anyone who interferes with their goal.

Both are willing to die in a fight over the same piece of property.

Participants in a custody battle often behave in a similar way.

From a financial point of view, the family who engages in a custody battle not only will need to divide its assets amongst itself, but now attorneys will take a significant percentage. Some custody cases can be settled for a few thousand dollars. Others go on for years and literally bankrupt the family. The stakes are high. It is no wonder, that some participants view the custody battle as a "fight to the death."

The loving parent who is convinced that his or her child will suffer by living with the other parent takes on a powerful motivation. Special feelings become aroused in a parent who perceives there is a "threat" to the future of one's offspring. Any loving, sheltering, and deeply committed parent who believes that adversity will face his or her child if he or she loses custody, is motivated to "fight like hell."

With these thoughts in mind, the participants in a custody battle must convince a Judge that he or she is the best parent to be the primary residential care-taker. In waging such a campaign, the parent wants the child to be convinced of this as well.

It is useful to think about the strategy that one uses in general when trying to convince somebody else to agree with you.

Simply put, there are two key points that must be established:

> First, you must convince the person you seek to persuade, that your adversary is bad.
>
> Second, you must convince the person you want to influence, that you are better.

The better job you do in convincing the Judge that you are the better parent and that your spouse is the inferior parent, increases the likelihood that you will win a custody battle.

What often transpires in a custody battle is that the participants believe that they have to convince *everyone* that they are the good parent and that the other one is the bad parent.

A nasty campaign is undertaken.

Neighbors become polarized.

Friends become divided.

The home community turns into a war zone.

Thus, one can see how something like parental alienation can come into play.

To make matters worse, the children involved are often fearful of losing one of the parents. In some cases, the children may fear losing both parents. Stressed, insecure, and unsure of their future, these children are even more vulnerable to others' manipulation of their own attitudes.

In the next Chapter, I will describe some of the alienating types of behavior that are engaged in by the parent intent on destroying a child's relationship with the opposite parent.

=9=

ALIENATING TECHNIQUES

In this Chapter, I will outline some of the alienating procedures used by various interfering parents in divorce. These examples come from the multitude of cases I have been exposed to, as well as the excellent writings of Dr. Gardner.

THE "DIRECT CRITICISM" TECHNIQUE

The first technique to be discussed, is simply called, "Direct Criticism."
In this method, the criticism may be aimed directly at the other parent such as, *"Your father is a bad man."* A direct criticism might be also be aimed at something associated with the other parent.
Consider the following:

> Bobby receives a gift from his mother. Bobby's father examines it and proclaims, *"she has terrible taste your mother, doesn't she?"*

In another example:

> While visiting at the father's home, Rosemary calls her mother and informs her that she and her dad went to see a particular movie. The mother replied, *"I can't believe your father took you to the one movie that every teacher has recommended that children not see."*

These types of behavior quickly achieve their purpose: the child learns that there is something "wrong" or "bad" with the other parent.

THE "IMPLIED CRITICISM" TECHNIQUE

A second procedure for alienating a child against a parent is the "Implied Criticism" method. Observe the following:

> A divorced man brings his son to his new finance's home. When the son returns to his mother she says, *"He took you to THAT woman's home?"*

In this example, the mother does not specifically attack the father or his fiance in a direct way. Instead, the mother *implies* that it is wrong for the father to take the child there and also *implies* that there is something bad about this woman.

To complicate the matter, the mother in this scenario may also believe that she has said nothing wrong because she did not *directly* attack either the ex-husband or his fiance.

When comments like these are made time after time, children learn relatively quickly *who* their parent and *what* their parent perceives as "good" and "bad." *To please the parent, sometimes the child will express the same attitude, even if the child does not really agree.*

THE "SARCASM" MANEUVER

Sarcasm is a powerful way to convey disapproval about something. It can attack bitterly, without directly saying so. Unfortunately, sarcasm is frequently used in the alienation of a child against a parent.

> William returned home with a new sportshirt and showed it to his mother. As she examined the shirt, she forced a laugh and said, *"So the big spender finally laid out some big bucks for you, huh?"*

Comments such as this rapidly teach a child that not only is the other parent "bad," but any gifts from that parent are "bad" as well.

THE "EXAGGERATION" PROCEDURE

Exaggeration is another technique often employed by a residential parent seeking to alienate a child from a nonresidential parent.

In this technique, negative claims about the noncustodial parent are blown way out of proportion. Some examples of this were provided earlier. The reader may recall how a mother who has an occasional after dinner drink is described to her children as an alcoholic.

Observe another example:

> A father who had legally reduced his child support payments was described to his son as a "cheat" who "deserved to be buried along with his *(the father's)* dead mother."

Or the following:

> A mother who was overheard appropriately disciplining her son was described as *"having a temper tantrum."*

Exaggeration can be a potent weapon in a campaign to alienate a child from a parent.

THE "REINTERPRETATION" STRATEGY

Another strategy that has been used to help alienate a child is the use of "reinterpretation." It is especially effective with younger children.

> Dawn cried because she missed her father. When her mother observed her crying she said to Dawn, *"I know how much he has hurt you."*

In another example:

> When Barry appeared to be more quiet than normal, he was told, *"Your mother has this effect on people."*

Children often have a hard enough time sorting out their feelings and coping with them. Many can be easily influenced. Parents who deliberately try to manipulate their children's feelings in this way, unfortunately may be quite successful.

THE "SCAPEGOATING" METHOD

Scapegoating also occurs all too frequently in the home designed to produce a Parental Alienation Syndrome. In this procedure, the noncustodial parent is blamed for anything the custodial parent cares to, even if the nonresidential parent had nothing to do with it.

A child whose grades had fallen was told that it was because of the other parent.

A mother who got a flat tire, explained to her children that their father refused to buy her "good tires."

A child who appeared sleepy at the father's home was questioned, *"Isn't your mother letting you get any sleep?"*

After numerous episodes of scapegoating, children come to understand that the nonresidential parent is viewed by the custodial parent as a bad person, who causes many bad things to happen. Eventually, the child may adopt the same attitude.

THE "GUILT INDUCTION" PROCEDURE

Many children in the custody of a parent who is trying to alienate the other parent are exposed to multiple guilt inducing manipulations.

A little girl expressed desire to visit with her father. Her mother replied, *"How can you leave me at a time like this?"*

While visiting with his father, Andrew telephoned his mother. Afterwards, he was asked by his father, *"How come you never want to call me?"*

Statements such as these basically ask the child for allegiance. Unfortunately, the allegiance is toward the alienation of the other parent.

THE "INTENTIONAL MANIPULATION" TECHNIQUE

The last alienating strategy to be discussed in this Chapter is the "Intentional Manipulation" technique. The range of such activities can vary tremendously.

A mother and child watched a scary movie on TV. When a close-up of a sinister character was presented in the movie, the mother buried her head in her lap, sighed several times and uttered repeatedly, "oh my god" in a disturbed manner. Startled and frightened, the child asked her what was wrong. The mother replied, *"That evil man in the movie reminds me of your father!"*

Consider this example:

Scotty's father deliberately bought a cereal that Scotty did not like. When the cereal was presented for Scotty to eat at breakfast, Scotty asked his father why he had bought this brand of cereal. Scotty's father replied, *"I'm sorry son, but your mother is taking all of my money, so I can only afford to buy the brands that are on sale."*

When one considers the range of techniques that are used to persuade a child to feel hostile toward the opposite parent, it becomes easy to see how a Parental Alienation Syndrome is actually accomplished.

= 10

DIVORCE RELATED MALICIOUS PARENT SYNDROME

Parental Alienation Syndrome is a terrible problem. However, in some cases, the problem is even worse.

Some custodial parents do not try just to alienate the other parent, but are intent on severely hurting that parent. Such efforts go beyond mere manipulation of the children.

I have been exposed to cases like this and have summarized these behaviors in an article which has been published in the *Journal Of Family Violence*. This abnormality is known as the "Divorce Related Malicious Parent Syndrome."

Individuals with Divorce Related Malicious Parent Syndrome are devoted to punishing the other parent, no matter what it takes.

Such spiteful parents have no problem lying, using others, or violating the law in order to achieve this purpose. Attempting to alienate the children from the other parent is only one aspect of the problem. Hurting that parent by whatever means necessary is the major mode of operation.

ATTACKING THE OTHER PARENT AND HIS OR HER PROPERTY

The viciousness that can be displayed in visitation interference situations can become quite serious. Observe the following examples:

One parent drove a car deliberately into the living room of the other parent's home.

One father arranged for radioactive waste to be dumped on his former spouse's lawn.

A father who had gained custody of his children had his house burned down by his ex-wife.

Actions such as these can result in serious injury, not only to the parent targeted, but to unintended individuals (such as the children for example) as well.

VICIOUS ALIENATING BEHAVIORS

The children of an individual who has Divorce Related Malicious Parent Syndrome are exposed to truly vicious attempts at alienating them from the other parent.

One mother told her daughter that her father was not really her father, even though he was.

One woman told her children that she could no longer buy food because all of the family's money was spent by their father on prostitutes at topless bars.

Another mother told her children that their father had physically abused her, even though he never had.

How can a child hearing these terrible things not be upset with the parent who purportedly committed these offenses? Such false accusations are potent instruments in the hands of a primary residential parent with Divorce Related Malicious Parent Syndrome.

THE ALIENATING TEAM

The kinds of behavior engaged in to alienate a child from his or her nonresidential parent can be quite powerful when the custodial parent is operating alone. However, parents suffering from Divorce Related Malicious Parent Syndrome involve many people in their battle against the former spouse.

One mother had her boyfriend beat up her ex-husband at times when he would come to try to visit with the children.

A custodial mother continuously informed her children and her own friends that the children's father was an "evil" man. She manipulated her friends to harrass him by openly following her ex-husband and the children when he picked them up for visitation.

One woman told her husband's boss that he was abusing the children on the premises of his work place.

Often, those persons who become part of the "Alienating Team" do not realize that they are being used in this way. Occasionally, a person may join the "Alienating Team" deliberately. Chapter 20 reviews some of the motivational factors that may come into play when such individuals decide to become involved in the alienation efforts.

VIOLATING THE LAW

As noted above, individuals suffering from Divorce Related Malicious Parent Syndrome may have no boundaries in their attacks upon the former marital partner. Violations of law are common.

A divorcing parent and friend put superglue into the locks of the car doors of the other divorcing parent so that not only would the other parent be unable to get his key into the car door locks, the locks would have to be replaced as well.

One father broke into the divorcing wife's new home and stole important papers.

To punish her divorced husband, a woman called the State

Abuse Registry and knowingly made a false accusation that he was sexually abusing their mutual child.

Like Parental Alienation Syndrome, there is no scientific research available on Divorce Related Malicious Parent Syndrome. Nevertheless, when one talks with parents, particularly in those cases where an intense custody battle is ongoing, these types of behaviors are described over and over again.

11

ABUSE ALLEGATIONS

One of the most devastating methods for interfering with visitation is to allege that a parent has sexually abused a child. Before going into what happens when someone is accused of sexually abusing a child, it is important to look at how common false allegations are made.

In his 1991 book on divorce, Dr. Hodges reviewed research of legal cases where custody or visitation disputes were at issue. Hodges reported that in those cases where a sexual abuse allegation was made, approximately 50 percent of the allegations were false.

In other words, *half of the cases in which a sexual abuse allegation was made were false.*

Why would someone make a false claim of sexual abuse of a child? There are two straightforward answers:

> In the first case, the accuser truly believes that the abuse has occurred and wants to protect the child.

> In the second case, the accuser believes that there is something to be gained by making the accusation.

What kind of benefits could there be for someone to make a false allegation of sexual abuse of a child? In a custody dispute, there are tremendous advantages for making such an accusation.

THE FALSE ALLEGATION

Consider the following scenario.

In the midst of a custody battle, a father receives a knock at the door and is greeted by state officials. They claim that someone has made a report accusing him of sexual abuse of his own child. In order to "protect the child," the state officials take the child from the father. The child is then handed over to the mother until a Hearing before a Judge can be arranged.

In this example, when the Hearing takes place, the Judge has two choices. First, the Judge can let the child go back with the father but runs the risk of the allegation being true. Thus, by letting the child go back with the father, the Judge may be failing to protect the child from sexual abuse.

The other choice is to keep the child away from the father until a "proper evaluation" can be done. In this scenario, the father in a way is treated as guilty; he must prove his innocence. This is the exact opposite of how we like to think our legal system operates.

In the United States of America, we are supposed to assume that some-one is innocent until proven guilty. But the actions in this case speak more toward the father having to prove his innocence. No doubt this is a difficult dilemma for a Judge. It is possible that an actual abuser could be set free. To "protect" the child, the father is restricted. His rights are limited. But what about the accuser?

At this point, I present the following case to help the reader grasp some of the issues involved.

THE CASE OF BRUCE AND LYDIA

Bruce and Lydia had a child. When the child was six months of age, Lydia left the home and Bruce became the primary residential parent. Bruce raised his little girl practically by himself. He changed her diapers, he fed her, he clothed her, he played with her, he read to her, and so on. As the years went by, those who knew Bruce and his daughter were impressed with the devotion and skill that this man displayed in bringing up his little girl.

One day when the daughter was five years old, state officials knocked on Bruce's door and told him that he had been accused of sexually abusing his daughter. The daughter was immediately taken away and placed with the daughter's biological mother. Lydia, had remarried and recently reappeared on the scene. It turned out that Lydia had changed her mind and now wanted to have custody of her daughter. She began to pursue this in Court.

The child was only allowed to visit with the father on occasion and only with supervision by someone else. She had lived with him all of her life. Now her father was a condemned man. She could only visit with him when someone else was watching.

As in most legal processes of this kind, the months dragged on and on. During this time period, the mother began trying to convince the child that she should live with the mother. To add to the difficulties, the mother's family insisted that the child was now claiming that the father had sexually abused the child. Remember the different techniques I talked about when I was discussing the Parental Alienation Syndrome? Remember the specific methods that can be used to manipulate a child's mind?

Lo and behold, the child began to claim that the father had "played a game" with her in the shower. Despite this, the child expressed continuous desire to spend time with the father. During the few restricted times that the child could see her father, she told him repeatedly that she wanted to live with him again.

The Court ordered a psychological evaluation. Without going into all of the details, the psychologist involved took four months to do this evaluation. I read the psychologist's report. It was clearly incompetent.

It was obvious to me that the person who had been Court ordered to do this evaluation of Bruce had very little if any experience in doing these things. The psychologist involved apparently had little knowledge of some of the scientific evidence that exists on sexual disorders (particularly what we refer to as heterosexual pedophilia: when an adult man is sexually aroused and active with little girls), children's claims of sexual abuse, and "experts" abilities to correctly identify who is and who isn't a sexual abuser.

The psychologist advised the Judge that even though no one could find any objective proof that sexual abuse had occurred, because the little girl had mentioned this "game" several times, the psychologist said that there was no way to guarantee her safety unless she was to live permanently with the mother. The psychologist further recommended that the father receive psychological treatment. Finally, the psychologist recommended that the little girl should only see the father under supervised conditions.

The result of this was that Bruce, an innocent man who had been falsely accused, who had raised his child and been the only parent his child knew for her first five years of life, was now viewed by outsiders as a sexual molester.

What did he do?
He ate 200 pills and tried to kill himself.

In this case, a mother obtained custody of her child by merely making a false accusation of sexual abuse of a child. An innocent man was accused of being guilty, treated as being guilty, and punished as being guilty, without any objective evidence.

So what happened to the accuser?

In this case, she got just what she wanted.

Unfortunately, as noted above, there is a high percentage of false accusations of sexual abuse made, particularly when a visitation and/or custody dispute is involved. It should also be noted that false accusations of abuse are not limited to sex. Or even the child.

In some cases, a parent may claim that the other parent has physically abused him or her, when in fact it never happened. A Judge may order that the accused parent must stay away from the accusing parent. And if there is a child involved, that may mean staying away from the child too. In some cases like this, the falsely accused parent may only be allowed to visit the child when someone (appointed by the Court) is there to supervise. In either case, a false accusation of physical abuse can result in visitation interference.

THE FALSE ACCUSER

When someone makes a false accusation of abuse, what happens if the accusation is investigated and determined to be "unfounded?"

Typically, nothing.

The person falsely accused tries to recover from the psychological, social, and financial trauma. The child continues to grow up. The accuser typically goes on with life as before. Rarely does the false accuser receive any punishment.

Some states have laws written which outline financial penalties and jail sentences for conviction of such offenses. Often these laws require proof that the false allegation was made with the knowledge that it was false. This can prove almost impossible to demonstrate, as long as the accuser has not admitted to anyone that the accusation was knowingly made as false.

Furthermore, the allegation of abuse has become so common in custody battles that some have come to view it as a minor violation. I have yet to see a case, particularly in a custody battle, where a false accuser was imprisoned.

=12

RELOCATION

An effective method for seriously interfering with visitation is to relocate one's residence far enough away from the other parent. When such a technique is employed, it creates a significant problem for the non-residential parent.

In this Chapter, I will describe four child relocation maneuvers. Each relocation maneuver described has generally the same goal, namely, to interfere with the visitation relationship between the child and nonresidential parent.

THE "DISTANCE RELOCATION"

In the "Distance Relocation," the primary aim of the custodial parent is to decrease access to the child by increasing the mileage between the primary residential home of the child and the home of the noncustodial parent. The range of the distance can vary considerably. In certain cases, a 20 minute drive will be increased to a 45 minute drive. In some spiteful cases, a custodial parent may move to another state just to interfere with the visitation rights of the former spouse.

THE "HARASSMENT RELOCATION"

Certain custodial parents seek not only to increase the distance between themselves and the ex-spouse, but also choose to relocate in a way that punishes a former marital partner. I label this maneuver the "Harassment Relocation."

In this approach to relocation, either the distance is increased or the new residence is one which is more hostile to the noncustodial parent.

A commonly chosen "harassment relocation" is for the residential parent to move in with his or her own parents. In this way, each time the visiting parent attempts to visit with the child, he or she now faces additional adversaries to deal with. Additionally, if the primary residential parent has moved in with relatives that are hostile to the noncustodial parent, the climate for the children becomes a more powerful system for attempts to alienate the children from the visiting parent.

THE "BANKRUPTCY RELOCATION"

A third relocation strategy is the "Bankruptcy Relocation." In this approach, the custodial parent moves to a residence that will teach the children that the other parent has financially "destroyed them all." A custodial parent may engage in this procedure even though there has been no major change in his or her economic status.

An extreme example of this manipulation is as follows.

A mother forced her children to sleep with her in a car to prove to them that their father had bankrupted them.

In this day and age in America, what could be a more powerful teacher than to be reduced to living out of an automobile?

KIDNAPPING

The most serious relocation maneuver is to kidnap a child. Approximately 350,000 children are kidnapped by a family member each year, according to the Department of Justice. The overwhelming majority of the kidnappers are parents of the children.

In a study which appeared in 1991 in the journal, *Social Work*, Drs. Hegar and Greif from the University of Maryland reported that 55% of the abductors were male. Drs. Hegar and Greif also found that 77% of the parents whose child was taken away, believed the kidnapping parent did it in order to hurt the former spouse.

In response to the severity of this problem, the United States Congress passed the Parental Kidnapping Act. This helped to set up certain government procedures to assist in attempts to find children who have been kidnapped.

One of these methods is the Federal Parent Locator Service. This service was originally designed to track down fathers who failed to provide Court Ordered child support payments ("Deadbeat Dads"). The Federal Parent Locator Service is housed within the Office of Child Support Enforcement. Parents trying to locate a kidnapped child can now access this important computerized network.

Various organizations are available to be of service to parents who are missing children. One of the most prominent organizations in this area is the National Center for Missing and Exploited Children.

Some of the more extreme kidnapping cases have achieved international headlines. Many might recall such a case in which a mother claimed that the father was sexually abusing the child; to protect the child, she moved secretly with the child to *another continent.*

The psychological issues that are created when a parent kidnaps a child are multiple and intense. Unfortunately, the problems do not easily go away after a kidnapped child is located. Further, in certain circumstances, the parent who kidnapped the child may actually achieve the intended goal even after being caught.

A woman had kidnapped her children and moved secretly thousands of miles away. The Federal government helped the father to locate his children. It took a long time. The case went to Court. The Judge ruled that the children should remain in the custody of their mother.

In this case, I was not aware of any evidence to suggest that the children's father was detrimental to his children in any way. My understanding is that the Judge felt that after all they had been through the "children needed their mother."

Needless to say, the father was devastated.

SECTION FOUR

NONCUSTODIAL ENCOURAGEMENT OF VISITATION INTERFERENCE

To this point, we have been discussing the negative qualities of a custodial parent who denies access to a child. Unfortunately, there are certain noncustodial parents who actually encourage the residential parent to interfere with visitation. As Dr. Kenneth Kressel once said of certain nonresidential Dads: "Divorced fathers are often their own worst enemies!"

In this Section, I would like to discuss several behaviors by which noncustodial parents may aggravate an existing visitation interference problem.

=13=

POOR JUDGMENT ACTIVITIES

When a noncustodial parent engages in abusive behavior toward the residential parent, this represents, at best, a display of poor judgment. This is especially so when one is already dealing with a visitation interference problem.

In this Chapter, I will briefly review some of the poor judgment engaged in by noncustodial parents as it relates to visitation interference. In the next Chapter, I will review preliminary research data on some of the types of abusiveness that may unfold.

VERBAL ABUSE

At her doorstep, a custodial mother was screamed at by the nonresidential father, demanding that she open the door. For safety reasons, the custodial mother remained inside the home with her child.

No one likes to be attacked verbally. It is even more upsetting when it becomes apparent that one cannot escape the verbal attacks.

When a noncustodial parent is verbally abusive of a residential parent at visitation transfers, this becomes self-defeating behavior.

On the one hand, the custodial parent wishes to follow the Court Ordered visitation schedule. On the other hand, the abused individual does not wish to be subjected to such verbal hostility.

These types of situations only spell trouble.

PHYSICAL ABUSE

One noncustodial father was abusive to the point of breaking into the residential parent's home to do what he wanted.

Domestic violence is a serious problem that affects both men and women.

Like the parent who verbally abuses the residential parent, the physically abusive parent only encourages visitation interference.

Why would anyone who gets physically abused when children are transferred wish to participate in such transfers? Interactions such as these are frightening to the victim herself and to the children involved.

Domestic violence is a major societial problem.

Fortunately, there has been increased attention to the problem in recent years, both in the popular media and in the professional literature. Treatment shelters, abuse hotlines and other clinical services devoted exclusively to domestic violence are now available across the country.

Our next chapter is devoted entirely to the problem of abusive behaviors.

SUBSTANCE ABUSE

A noncustodial father repeatedly came to visit with his child so drunk that the Court Ordered for all visitation to be supervised.

Noncustodial parents who abuse alcohol or drugs when visiting their children pose a significant problem.

Again, engaging in this type of behavior puts the custodial parent in a no win situation. If she allows the substance abusing individual to spend time with the child without supervision, the child may be at risk for harm. On the other hand, if she denies the visitation, she may be violating the child's right of access to the other parent.

The best remedy for this situation is the most obvious one: the noncustodial parent needs to be treated so that he or she can refrain from any substance abuse.

FAILURE TO FOLLOW GUIDELINES

A noncustodial father was required to return his daughter at a particular time. He did not. Instead, he kept her for additional time without consulting the custodial mother. When he finally returned the child, he claimed that he and the daughter were having such a good time that he did not want to "deny her" this opportunity.

One could say that this example represents a "minor" violation of good "visitation etiquette." Yet when a nonresidential parent violates the visitation guidelines, it teaches the custodial parent several things.

First, it basically says, "There is no need to follow the guidelines." This might encourage the custodial parent to also violate the guidelines.

Additionally, by not following the guidelines, the noncustodial parent is providing evidence that he or she is not reliable in this area. This is not only a bad message for the child, but could come to haunt the noncustodial parent later when appealing to a Judge for help with access to the child.

Everyone benefits when the visitation schedule is followed. To violate it, only encourages more problems and may in fact worsen a visitation interference pattern established by the other parent.

NON-PAYMENT OF CHILD SUPPORT

One of the major areas that has received media attention in the divorce and post-divorce dispute situation is the phenomenon of the "Deadbeat Dad." Failure to pay Court Ordered child support is a serious problem. It hurts the children, it hurts the custodial parent, and it hurts society as well.

There is some evidence to suggest that there is a relationship between visitation frequency and child support payments in certain cases. The exact nature of the relationship is not clear. In fact, a 1993 study by Jonathan Veum of the Office of Economic Research at the U.S. Bureau of Labor Statistics, suggested that when looking at a large number of cases, there may not be a relationship between child support and visitation frequency.

I suspect that if one is to look at situations where visitation interference exists, there is a greater likelihood of seeing a relationship between visitation frequency and child support payment.

Some parents who are denied visitation, feel no need to pay the child support they have been Court Ordered to provide. So they don't. Unfortunately, this may also encourage the parent not receiving the Court Ordered child support to become even more interfering in the visitation situation.

The battle may escalate quickly.

The Courts generally behave in such a way that child support and visitation are considered to be separate issues. In many states, one cannot legally deny visitation because the other parent has failed to pay child support. On the other hand, the parent who has not received any financial support that has been Court Ordered for the child, may feel justified to not allow that parent to have access to the child.

Even though the child support and visitation issues are considered separate in most Courtrooms, the parent who fails to pay the Court Ordered child support may help the Judge develop a negative attitude toward that parent. This may come to backfire on the non-paying parent. A Judge may be less likely to assist the non-paying parent when he is complaining of visitation interference.

BAD-MOUTHING THE CUSTODIAL PARENT

A noncustodial father told his daughter that his mother did not really love her. The daughter's response was to reduce her time spent with her father.

Can you imagine this poor child's reaction? Her father had just shot an arrow through her little heart.

What could she say?

What could she do?

By attacking the mother, the father not only hurt his little girl, he also hurt his own relationship with his daughter.

Unjustifiably attacking the other parent is abusive of both the child and parent involved.

Verbally attacking the custodial parent to the child clearly places the child in a no win situation. Additionally, the residential parent who becomes aware of such attacks is placed in a difficult dilemma.

Such behavior can only encourage any tendencies in the primary residential parent toward visitation interference.

DENYING THE CHILDREN'S NEEDS

A noncustodial mother lived in a town neighboring where the primary residential father resided. During her visitation period, she refused to allow the child to participate in school related social activities, which were important to the child. This pattern encouraged the child to eventually refuse to visit with the noncustodial mother.

The nonresidential parent who does not attend to the needs of his or her own children is only encouraging potential visitation interference.

In a divorce situation, the needs of the children are paramount. When a noncustodial parent ignores those needs or abuses those children, he or she is only encouraging the other parent (and in some cases, the children) to engage in visitation interference.

THE INTERPERSONALLY DYSFUNCTIONAL PARENT

Earlier I noted a comment by Dr. Kressel regarding certain noncustodial fathers in which he said, "Divorced fathers are often their own worst enemies!" This was Dr. Kressel's conclusion after studying a sample of divorce mediation cases. While the individuals that Dr. Kressel studied are most likely not representative of the typical father in a divorce, nevertheless there are some lessons to be learned from examining this small group.

In a case study of a small group of fathers, Dr. Kressel noted that many of them displayed certain inappropriate behaviors. These included the following:

Preoccupation with their own needs over the children's.
A negative or irresponsible attitude toward the other parent's needs.
Encouraging the children to disrespect the other parent.
Denial of any part in the conflict with the other parent.

In his 1988 article which appeared in the *Journal of Family Psychology,*

Dr. Kressel found that these fathers often did not have a genuine wish to be involved with their children.

Clearly, a parent who engages in these types of behaviors may indeed be encouraging the other parent to engage in visitation interference.

=== 14 ===

ABUSIVE BEHAVIORS

A surefire way to encourage visitation interference by a custodial parent is to abuse such a person when dealing with the children.

Unfortunately, some noncustodial parents are quite abusive of their former spouses.

At the present time, we do not know the extent to which visitation interference is generated by the abusiveness of the nonresidential parent toward the custodial parent. However, in 1993, Melanie Shepard published a paper in the journal, *Child Welfare*, which addresses certain aspects of this problem. Using her report, I will outline some of the major types of abusive behavior engaged in by noncustodial fathers. I will also report on some of the major abusive behaviors displayed by custodial mothers.

Before doing so however, it is important to mention a few key points to consider when reviewing this useful report by Dr. Shepard.

THE PARENTS INVOLVED

Dr. Shepard conducted an exploratory study with families who had a history of domestic abuse. The subjects were 25 custodial mothers and 22 non-residential fathers. All but one of the families were Court Ordered to use a center designed for dealing with domestic abuse and child visiting.

The center served as a neutral transfer point for child visitation. In some cases, the actual visitation took place at the center.

All 22 noncustodial fathers and 3 custodial mothers had a Restraining Order placed upon them because of domestic abuse.

There was a significant amount of physical abuse reported by both mothers and fathers. Over 90% of the mothers in the study said that their former husband had physically abused them; 45% of the fathers said that their former wife had physically abused them.

I raise these issues so that the reader will be aware that this study is of a select group of people. The reader should not assume that the study represents the typical situation between a set of divorced parents.

PSYCHOLOGICAL ABUSE OF CUSTODIAL MOTHERS

Below I review some of the major findings from interviewing the 25 custodial mothers about psychological abuse imposed upon them by the nonresidential fathers. These behaviors were considered to be frequently occurring:

67% received criticism about their friends or relatives
46% were threatened with legal action to change custody
46% received angry looks
46% were made to do something humiliating
42% were demanded to produce the children independent of the visitation schedule

Clearly, these types of behaviors by noncustodial fathers would only serve to encourage the primary residential parent to seek to avoid them whenever possible. Given that there are children involved, it is very easy to see how psychologically abusive behavior by a noncustodial parent could lead to a deterioration in access to the children involved.

PHYSICAL ABUSE OF CUSTODIAL MOTHERS

Like the data on psychological abuse, the mothers with primary residential custody also were subjected to physical abuse.

42% reported being pushed or grabbed
42% said they were slapped or punched
37% said their sexual body parts were attacked
37% reported being physically restrained

What can possibly be said about such behavior? Clearly, no parent or child should be subjected to such events.

ABUSE OF NONCUSTODIAL FATHERS

The 22 fathers participating in this study reported that the following behaviors by the custodial mothers occurred frequently:

61% said they were criticized in front of the children
56% reported being threatened with further Court ordered visitation restriction
52% said they were refused the opportunity for joint decision-making about the children
52% claimed they were not allowed to see their children

These findings document some of the types of abuse that are seen in certain child visitation interference situations.

Throughout the pages you have read so far, a whole range of abusive behaviors have been described. Some parents are just downright vicious.

They lie to their children.

They cheat their kids of the other parent's comfort.

They manipulate others to hurt their own children.

Such despicable actions take their toll. It's time we discuss how children react to these sinister actions.

SECTION FIVE

THE CHILDREN'S REACTIONS

In this Section of the book, I will review some of the ways that children react to visitation interference.

It should be noted that there is an absence of scientific research on the precise responses that children have when exposed to interference of visitation. This should come as no surprise given the fact that child visitation interference in general has not received much scientific attention. In any event, I will describe many of the reactions that children have from my own observations as well as those anecdotal reports that appear in the professional literature.

Chapter 15 will review some of the passive responses of children to visitation interference.

Chapter 16 will discuss some of the active responses that children have to denied parental access.

Chapter 17 will discuss changes in children that may be seen over time.

Lastly, it is important for the reader to keep in mind that children can have both passive and active responses to child visitation interference. How one child responds may be quite different from how another child responds. Over time, the same child can show significant changes as well in responding to visitation interference.

= 15

PASSIVE RESPONSES OF CHILDREN

In certain situations, children may have reactions to child visitation interference which are not obvious to others. These responses are relatively passive in nature. They are the basis of this Chapter.

POWERLESSNESS

A mother screams at the top of her lungs to her ex-husband, "You will never see Billy again!" The ex-husband replies at the top of his lungs, "I'll make sure you burn in Hell before that happens!"

This is a terrible thing for a little child to be exposed to.

Now I ask you, what can the 8 year old boy observing this interaction of his parents do? In many instances of child visitation interference, the child is virtually powerless.

As in this example.

What 8 year old boy can stand up to a grown man who has the "power" to make his mother "burn in Hell?"

What 8 year old boy can control a grown woman who screams with such intensity and unyielding authority?

When a child is told that he or she will not be allowed to visit with the other parent, what can such a child do?

In most cases, at the moment that the edict is handed down to the child, the child has basically no power over the situation. The child capitulates.

Powerlessness is rarely a pleasant emotion.

INTIMIDATION

Related to the feeling of powerlessness, is the experience of intimidation. Observe the following example:

Susie is a 9 year old girl of average height and weight. Her father is 35 years old. He is 6' 2" and weighs 210 pounds. Susie wants to call her mother but knows that her father will be very angry if she expresses that desire. When the issue of calling the mother comes up, Susie would like to tell her father how she really feels about it. She cannot bring herself to do it.

Such is the experience of intimidation in visitation interference.

In this example, the child would appear to experience powerlessness and intimidation. However, it should be noted that the two can operate independently.

For example, a child may not feel intimidated to the point of keeping his or her feelings inside, but nonetheless may feel powerless in the situation. In other words, a child may make a request to visit with the other parent which is then flatly refused by the custodial parent.

Thus, though not intimidated, in this example the child is still powerless.

ANGER

Joey is a 7 year boy who has not been allowed to see his father in weeks. He misses him dearly. He wants to be with him badly. He listens to his mother rant and rave about what an "evil" person his father is. Joey has come to realize that his mother is preventing him from seeing his father. Joey is angry.

Many children like Joey will experience this type of anger. However, many children, particularly those that are intimidated or powerless, will be unable to do anything about their anger. Some will hide it. Some will display it in other ways. Others, as we shall see in Chapter 16, will display it outwardly.

DEPRESSION

In visitation interference situations, it is not uncommon for a child to experience symptoms of depression. Crying, withdrawal, irritability, sleep disturbance, loss of appetite, fatigue, hopelessness, and poor functioning are some of the symptoms children may experience.

One child may become quiet.

A second child may overeat.

A third child may complain of constant stomach pains.

A fourth child may tell her brother "in secret" that she wants to die.

Each of these examples may represent depression that results from visitation interference. While there are similarities from case to case, there may be significant differences from case to case as well.

SADNESS

Some children may not develop a full blown depression from visitation interference. Some may just develop an understandable sadness.

Being unable to see a loved parent is a difficult thing to cope with, even for an adult. The child who has lost that parent is likely to be sad.

To make matters worse, often when a child is cut off from a parent, he or she is also cut off from that parent's relatives and friends. Many of these individuals may have been important, rewarding persons for that child. Such losses naturally produce sadness.

SELF BLAME

It is not uncommon in a divorce situation for children to blame themselves. This is also true for visitation interference.

AnnMarie has not been allowed to see her father for three months. Whenever AnnMarie brings up her father's name, her mother becomes hostile and belligerent. After a while, AnnMarie may begin to wonder if she herself has caused this problem. She may tell herself, *"AnnMarie is a bad girl,"* as an explanation for the absence of the father.

Some children may blame themselves in the following way: *"What did I do to cause daddy not to see me?"* In this instance, the child is searching for a reason but does not wish to blame the custodial parent.

In some of the more disturbed custodial parents' homes, the child may have to display dislike for the nonresidential parent in order to be allowed to visit with him or her. Acting in this way, the child may eventually adopt the notion that it is the child's fault that the visiting parent cannot be seen.

BODILY COMPLAINTS

One of the common passive responses of children to visitation interference is to complain of medical related problems. In my experience, headaches and stomach pains are among some of the most common symptoms.

The child who cannot say to an angry vindictive parent, *"I want to see my daddy,"* can say, *"My stomach is killing me."*

The child who frequently complains of medical ailments, will eventually become known to the family physician or pediatrician. A good medical doctor, in time, will recognize that the complaints are not of medical origin.

Hopefully, the physician might be able to address the basic cause of the child's problem.

LOVE

Tommy is 11 years old. Two months ago, his father moved out and filed for divorce. Prior to the separation, Tommy had a loving relationship with both parents. In response to Tommy's father leaving the home, Tommy's mother has not allowed him to visit with his father. She has told Tommy how, "he has abandoned us." Tommy's father calls every day trying to speak to Tommy but his mother will not allow it. Tommy sees his father come to the home every other day and tries to see him, which his mother will not allow. Every time Tommy brings up his father's name, his mother gets angry.

How can a little boy who has loved his father for eleven years of his life, suddenly abandon his love for him, especially when the father has not done anything to directly hurt the child?

The answer is: he can't.

In many child visitation interference situations, the child must learn to hide his or her love from the parent who interferes with the visitation. This does not mean that love no longer exits; it just means that the love may have to be covert. A secret love. A love that can only be expressed when actually allowed.

INSECURITY

Children who have lost contact with a parent through visitation interference often may experience an increase in feelings of insecurity. A child may learn rather quickly that if a big strong adult can be banished from his or her home, *"What can happen to me?"*

Some children may cling more to the residential parent. Having lost one parent, the child may frantically try to please the residential parent and stay as close by as possible.

Other children may demonstrate their insecurity in different ways.

Attention getting ploys may be seen.

A fear of the dark may develop at bedtime.

Actions designed to elicit reassurance may become common.

A desire to sleep with the residential parent may unfold.

Avoidance of being alone may occur.

While commonly experienced among children who have been denied access to a loving parent, insecure feelings may reveal themselves in different ways.

ACADEMIC DETERIORATION

The last passive response to be discussed in this Chapter concerns how the child may perform at school.

The child stressed by the absence of a loved parent may become less motivated and interested in school work.

Some children may have difficulty concentrating which may or may not be noticed by teachers.

Homework may become ignored.

Deadlines may be forgotten.

The parent who does not actively attend to the child's ongoing school performance, may not learn of the problem until the report card comes. By that point, it may prove very difficult to turn things around in a short time period.

THE PASSIVE RESPONSES

Powerlessness. Intimidation. Anger. Depression. Secret love for the absent parent. These are some of the passive responses that children may display when denied access to a nonresidential parent. In the next Chapter, we will introduce some of the active responses of children facing the dilemma of child visitation interference.

=16=

ACTIVE RESPONSES
OF CHILDREN

Children are survivors. Make no mistake about it. *How* they survive
is the key issue.

In certain instances, passive responses work well. However, in other
situations, a child may react more actively in dealing with visitation
interference. In this section, I will outline some of the active responses
seen in children involving visitation and custody disputes.

Before outlining some of these responses, the reader needs to be aware
that each child has his or her own unique way of responding. Some children may be purely passive whereas others may be more active. Even
those who are more active may have very different approaches. Many
children demonstrate both passive and active reactions. In any event, the
reader should find the following descriptions to be useful.

THE CARETAKING CHILD

In certain cases of child visitation interference, the custodial parent
conveys to the child that the child's help is needed. Often, the custodial
parent may present oneself as more vulnerable and hurting than the nonresidential parent.

When a child with a natural tendency to "take care of others" sees his
or her parent crying, angry, lethargic, or acting in other discomforted
ways, such a child may feel compelled to do whatever is necessary to "help"
that parent.

Unfortunately, sometimes the child is led to the conclusion that not visiting with the nonresidential parent will "help" the residential parent.

In these types of situations, the child may take a very active role in contributing to the visitation interference initiated by the custodial parent. The child may:

refuse to leave the "ill" parent home alone;
blame the visiting parent for the other parent's condition;
refuse to interact with the nonresidential parent.

In extreme cases, the child may create terrible stories about the visiting parent to provide a "compelling" justification for not visiting with that parent.

THE MANIPULATIVE CHILD

In many families, children may actively manipulate one or both parents to gain certain advantages. For example, some children will make statements such as, "*But Daddy always buys me that!*" Such a comment suggests to the mother that she is "failing" in some way. The same child may tell the father that, "Mommy always lets me do that."

Such manipulative tactics may be seen frequently in families involving divorce. When such families also have an ongoing visitation interference dispute, these manipulative efforts may be utilized as well.

Children manipulating in this way may utter statements such as, "*Why should I go visit with Daddy when he won't buy me anything?*" Comments such as these appear like "music to the ear" of a custodial parent who is intent on interfering with visitation. The interfering parent who hears such manipulative words from his or her child is very likely to reward the child for this type of behavior.

THE GUILT-TRIPPING CHILD

Another active coping strategy of certain children in visitation interference situations is to try to induce feelings of guilt in the parent involved. When finally able to speak to the parent being prevented from visiting, the child may state, "*Don't you love me anymore?*"

Sometimes, the child who tries to use guilt will unsuccessfully attempt such an effort with the visitation preventing custodial parent. For example, the child may tell the custodial parent, *"If you really love me you would make sure that I could see Mommy."* Unfortunately, such statements often fall on deaf ears as the interfering custodial parent might retort, *"I have tried and tried but she is uncooperative"* (despite the falsity of this statement).

THE ACTING OUT CHILD

Visitation deprivation can often lead to serious "acting out" behaviors.

Horace throws a temper tantrum.
Cherie steals a box of candy from the 7-11 store.
Carl bullies the smaller children in his class.

The key is that the acting out child is frustrated and is trying to draw attention to the problem that he or she is experiencing. Unfortunately, the custodial parent of such a child who is intent on disturbing the relationship between the child and the visiting parent, will often use the acting out behavior as a means to further the alienation campaign. For example, when the child is throwing a temper tantrum the custodial parent might claim, *"See what his mother has done to him!"*

THE CUSTODY BATTLE CHILD

While children in a custody battle may exhibit any of the passive and active responses noted above, there is a unique set of demands placed upon these children.

Two parents are vying for the child's "vote" as to whom the child would prefer to live with. Whether aware of it or not, both parents exert pressure on the child in this regard. If the pressure becomes very intense, the child may literally feel "ripped apart."

Some of the active strategies in coping may be similar to the ones described above, but such children must also respond to the friends and family of each parent; these other adults are also likely to be putting some degree of pressure on the child.

Some children in a custody battle may find that they have to tell each parent what the child thinks each parent wants to hear, even if it amounts to contradictory statements. Some children will go as far as to outwardly lie in order to accommodate what he or she thinks the parent wants to hear.

In some respects, trying to meet the demands of each parent forces the child to act like a politician dealing with hostile forces. Whereas the child used to be able to act in a spontaneous, carefree manner, now he or she must calculate what to say or do.

In this sense, it might appear that the custody battle child is forced to lose part of the innocence and enthusiasm of childhood. In it's place comes a guarded skepticism often seen in the experienced politician.

THE PENALIZED CHILD

In certain visitation interference situations, the child continues to express the desire to see the visiting parent but the custodial parent continues to prevent it. In some cases, the custodial parent will literally punish the child for expressions of affection toward the nonresidential parent. In other situations, the child may be ridiculed in front of his or her siblings. Favoritism may be demonstrated as well.

Observe the following example:

> In one custody battle case, the eldest of three children made his preference known that he wanted to live with his father. The mother's response was to tell the boy in front of the other children, "You're just like your father.... you deserve each other.... you're both sickos."

Experiences like these may produce a variety of active responses in the child.

Rona curses and screams.
Harry runs away from home.
Vickie refuses to speak to the attacking parent.

In either case, the penalized child bears a heavy burden for desiring to be with the nonresidential parent whose access has been denied.

THE ALIENATED CHILD

In cases of full-blown Parental Alienation Syndrome, a child may take a very active approach toward contributing to the visitation denial situation. Some parents are successful at "shaping up" their children to view the nonresidential parent with such disgust and anger, that the child actively avoids visitation.

In many such cases, the pressure placed upon the child to hate the other parent is enormous. Fearful of losing the custodial parent as well, the child does everything he or she can to please the custodial parent. This may include acting like he or she hates the nonresidential parent, even though this parent is deeply loved.

The child may scream and yell about how he or she does not want to see the other parent, even though there is no legitimate reason. In some extreme cases, the child may even fabricate physical or sexual abuse as the reason in order to satisfy the custodial parent's desire for visitation interference.

THE ACTIVE RESPONSES

Manipulation. Guilt-tripping. Screaming. Cursing. Temper tantrums. Running away from home. As we can see, the range of active responses by children to visitation interference is wide.

17

THE EVOLVING CHILD

As children grow, their attitudes and behaviors will change as well. Such is true for the child who has been denied access to the nonresidential parent.

The child at age eight who has been denied access may carry on emotionally but after several years of visitation prevention, he or she will often adjust to the one parent situation. The adjustment may or may not be good.

Temper tantrums may be replaced by inner anger at the custodial parent. Longing for the visiting parent may be replaced by anger for abandonment. The key point is that over time the feelings, attitudes, and behaviors of such children will evolve.

Related to the above, the sex of the child plays an important role in the evolution.

The relationship between a five year old daughter and her father will naturally change as she goes through puberty and develops into a young woman. When one adds in a visitation interference element to such development, all kinds of changes can take place.

Some girls will become increasingly shy.

Others may become quite attention seeking.

Some may become sexually peoccupied.

What exactly happens to children who have been denied access to a parent when the children grow up?

Unfortunately, most of what we know comes from stories from the wounded. We await the development of a sound body of scientific research in this area.

My own exposure to clinical and legal cases, as well as my reading of various reports in the professional literature, tells me there are certain areas that require comment.

Children react differently to divorce over time. The same is true for their reactions over time to denied visitation.

Some will cope well.

Many will cope poorly.

Below I will comment on several key areas.

MEMORIES

As the years go on, children who have been denied access to a parent, may have changes in their memories of the parent they are missing.

Some children over time may hold onto whatever actual memories they had. Good memories may become even better in fantasy.

Some memories may be lost forever. I suspect this may be more true for the very young person who was denied parental visitation for many years. Older children are probably less likely to lose memories of the visitation deprived parent.

In certain cases, children will create fantasies about the missing parent. These fantasies may eventually become part of the "memories" of the visitation denied parent.

PSYCHOLOGICAL PROBLEMS

As mentioned earlier, how children cope with divorce and visitation denial differs among children and may also differ in the same children over time.

Some may require therapy early in the family breakup. Others may require treatment later in life. Some will not require intervention of any kind.

While there is an absence of research on how children cope when denied access to a parent, a 1992 study by Drs. Greif and Hager which was published in the *American Journal of Orthopsychiatry*, sheds some light on the issue. Drs. Greif and Hager reviewed the literature on abducted children. These authors found that the children's reactions varied from each other and over time.

For those children who experienced psychological difficulties, Drs.

Greif and Hager reported that the longer the child was separated from the denied parent, the more problems the child had. Furthermore, the researchers also noted that abducted children who were forced to undergo long periods of visitation denial, found the denied parental access to have had a "negative and continuing impact on their lives."

Many readers will not be too suprised by these findings.

RELATIONSHIP WITH THE DENIED PARENT

In my experience, as the child grows older, sooner or later he or she will seek out the parent that has been denied access.

In certain situations, there will be anger toward the parent for "not trying hard enough" even if that parent did try, and even if her or she tried exhaustively.

In other situations, the child will be relieved and gratified to re-establish the connection.

There are so many factors that come into play that it is impossible to predict all of the types of reactions that one may see. Nevertheless, I have seen various individuals who despite having been physically abused by a parent during childhood, at some point in life return to that parent and try to come to some resolution of it.

Unfortunately, it may not be easy to repair the damage done.

RELATIONSHIP WITH THE PARENT DENYING VISITATION

As the child grows older, what happens to the parent who has caused the visitation interference ?

I have spoken to some adults who have went through custody battles and went through visitation interference when they were children. Depending on the circumstances involved, the relationship between the child and the denied parent will vary. However, in cases of attempted alienation, if the other parent has previously been a good parent, when the child grows up, he or she may hold a tremendous anger at the custodial parent for depriving both the child and the nonresidential parent of the years of childhood together.

Forgiving the visitation denying parent may prove too difficult for some adults who were subject to losing years of childhood with a loving parent.

RELATIONSHIPS WITH OTHERS

The child who has experienced long periods of being denied access to a parent may have difficulty in certain relationships with others. It may also affect the way such an individual may act as a parent later on in life.

There is some evidence available that certain abusing adults had a parent that was abusive toward them during childhood. Is the child who was denied visitation likely to grow up to deny visitation to one's own child?

Unfortunately, I suspect this will be true for some.

However, I have been told by some adults who were denied visitation as children, that they would never allow their offspring to endure such pain.

REACTIONS OF THE DENIED PARENT

An important point to consider in discussing the evolution of a child who has visitation interference experiences, is the way in which the denied parent has coped.

Some parents find the experiences so painful that they decide to totally divorce themselves from the family situation. Others cling on in an emotional way, taking blow by blow but "hanging in there" until the child becomes "emancipated."

The bitter parent may make it more difficult for the child.

The selfish parent may find the child remains detached.

At the present time, we are in dire need of good research data on this issue. Nevertheless, it seems relatively safe to conclude that how the parent copes with the denied visitation, will play an important role in how the child evolves in this process.

SECTION SIX

LEGAL ISSUES

In this Section, the reader will be introduced to a variety of important legal issues that surface when one is dealing with a visitation and/or custody dispute.

Chapter 18 provides an overview of the judicial system as it relates to visitation and custody disputes.

Chapter 19 discusses how to go about selecting an attorney.

=18

THE JUDICIAL SYSTEM

Disputes about visitation inevitably end up in the Courtroom. This Chapter will review some of the major issues involved with legal actions aimed at managing child visitation interference. For practical answers about the judicial system, I recommend that the reader speak with his or her attorney. I am not an attorney and I do not profess to be providing legal advice in this book.

For simplicity, I will divide this Chapter into three sections. The first section will discuss aspects of the process that one goes through when the Court becomes involved in a visitation dispute. Next, I will briefly discuss the role of the attorneys. This portion on attorneys will be limited in scope as Chapter 19 focuses on this topic in depth. The last section of Chapter 18 will address the role of the Judge.

THE JUDICIAL PROCESS

Once a visitation dispute appears unsolvable outside of the Courtroom, then a Motion will be made to be heard by a Judge. In the overwhelming majority of such situations, the Motion is made by an attorney and a response to that Motion will be provided by the attorney representing the other party. Eventually, a Hearing date will be set and both attorneys will present the case to the Judge who will make a decision about the Motion under consideration.

Visitation disputes typically are covered in the following four areas:

Final Judgment
Modification of the Final Judgment

Enforcement Motion
Contempt Motion

Before discussing each of these, it is important that I review certain "tools" at the attorney's disposal which are often used in visitation and custody disputes.

PRE-HEARING DISCOVERY

Once a Motion has been filed, your attorney will prepare his or her case for the upcoming Hearing before the Judge.

You and your attorney will discuss the issues in depth.

You will provide the attorney with whatever evidence you have.

You will be asked some questions that you probably cannot answer.

You may have witnesses that need to be called.

All of this effort is known as "trial preparation." It is in your best interest for the attorney who represents you to be as well prepared as possible for a Courtroom appearance.

When you have witnesses that you would like to be called to the stand, if you believe they will be favorable to you then your attorney will most likely call the person on the telephone or set up a meeting. The attorney who does this, helps to reduce "surprises" in the Courtroom. The last thing the attorney wants is to call a witness who then provides information against you.

There are times when the opposing side is likely to call a witness who will be hostile to your case. Or, there is a witness about whom you are not sure what his or her testimony will be. In these situations, the attorney has a "discovery" tool which can be used. It is known as a deposition and I will discuss it in just a moment.

Similarly, at times there may be information in certain documents that is useful in a visitation dispute Hearing. Sometimes these documents are easy to obtain. At other times, they may not be easily accessed. Your attorney has at his or her disposal another discovery tool known as the subpoena. Your attorney would like to "discover" what this evidence is *before* the actual Hearing. This activity is referred to as (pre-hearing or pre-trial) "discovery."

Let me now discuss the deposition and subpoena options that can be used during discovery.

DEPOSITION

In a deposition, a witness is notified that he or she must come to a certain place at a certain time to answer questions by your attorney. The attorney representing the other side will also be notified of this deposition. You and your former spouse can both attend the deposition.

Typically, the deposition is taken in one of the attorney's offices. A Court reporter is usually hired to transcribe the questions and answers given. The person being deposed will be sworn in to give testimony. He or she may bring an attorney as well.

During the deposition, the attorneys will ask questions and the individual being deposed will answer them. However, the person being deposed can refuse to answer questions.

Whatever is said in the deposition, is transcribed. It is fully admissible in the Courtroom. In a visitation dispute situation, certain depositions can prove to be very useful.

For example, a neighbor who has observed the opposing parent try to prevent you from having access to your child, may be very reluctant to get involved. However, if the neighbor is deposed by your attorney, his or her testimony is now available for the Judge to hear.

In another example, a person who may be hostile to your case might change his or her story from the time he or she is deposed to the time the person appears at the Hearing in front of the Judge. When an individual changes his or her story, having the deposition transcripts available to present in Court, enables your attorney to demonstrate to the Judge that the witness has changed his or her testimony. This enables your attorney to discredit the witness in front of the Judge. The person who has changed his or her story can simply be asked, "were you lying then or are you lying now"?

It's a pretty powerful question.

By demonstrating the testimony of an adversarial witness to be unreliable, your attorney has helped reduce the importance of that witness to the Judge.

These are just some of the types of the scenarios in which a deposition can be useful.

SUBPOENA

Assume that your former spouse has a friend that is trying to assist in alienating your child from you. In a deposition, this friend has denied seeing your child in months. You know that this friend has lately been going to see your child at school. Both you and your attorney decide that it is important for you to obtain the school sign-in sheets for visitors which document who comes into the school, on which days, and at what times.

You try to obtain the information from the school but they tell you that they are not permitted to give the sign-in sheets out. They also tell you that they are not permitted to make copies of the sign-in sheets. How can you obtain them?

Your attorney can issue a subpoena which requires them to bring the documents in question to the attorney's office at a certain date and time.

There are many applications for the use of a subpoena. Someone may have videotaped your former partner preventing your child from being with you. You ask the person for a copy of the tape but your request is refused. Do not despair: your attorney can subpoena it.

Similarly, you become aware of a letter written by your ex-spouse to the coach of your son's little league baseball team. This letter tells the coach that you are not permitted to know what your son's baseball team schedule is. The coach would like to give you the letter but is afraid that if he does, your spouse will take it out on him. In such a situation, a subpoena will come in very handy. When confronted by your ex-spouse, the coach can claim, *"it wasn't up to me...I got subpoenaed"!*

Once your attorney has completed his or her preparation for the Hearing, including depositions, subpoenas, and any other means available, you are now ready to have a Hearing.

HEARING

As I mentioned earlier, there are at least four different types of Hearings that are important in visitation disputes. I will discuss each type in just a moment. However, before doing so, the reader may have noticed that I have delayed talking about these four types of Hearings on two occasions in this Chapter. I have done so deliberately.

The key word here is *delay*. And it can become frustrating. Unfortunately, that is the way the judicial system operates.

You walk into an attorney's office upset that you cannot see your daughter. She assures you that it will be no problem to correct this difficulty. A Motion is filed. Two weeks go by before the opposing attorney files a response. Your attorney deposes your former spouse. Your ex-spouse has his attorney depose you. You subpoena school records. You depose your daughter's teacher and tennis instructor. Weeks go by. Paper work between the attorneys fly. You speak with your attorney on the phone week after week. Before you know it, four months have elapsed and you still have not seen your daughter. Finally, tomorrow you will have a Hearing before the Judge.

Get the picture?

The process is slow and it is frustrating.

Now that you've had a small taste of "delay," let's discuss those different types of Hearings.

THE FINAL JUDGMENT

When a married couple gets divorced, visitation with the children will be spelled out in the Final Judgment (also referred to as the Final Decree). Issues of child support, alimony, asset distribution, and custody will be addressed as well. Further, who will be responsible to pay what bills will be included in the Final Judgment.

Once the Final Judgment is made, it is difficult to change it. Modifications to the Final Judgment can be made, but they are usually not easily accomplished.

There is a good reason for this.

After a case has been tried, Judges do not wish to try it again. Otherwise, the Courtrooms would be even more backed up than they are now. If every Final Decree could be easily modified, then there would be no need for a Final Decree.

Thus, if you are provided certain visitation rights in the Final Judgment and you are not happy with them, your attorney might recommend that you file an Appeal. Unfortunately, the success rate of Appeals is incredibly low.

Another alternative that your attorney might recommend is to let some time elapse and then consider filing a "Motion for Modification."

MODIFICATION MOTIONS

In the Hearing for Modification, you must demonstrate that certain key circumstances have changed which require that the appropriate portion of the Final Judgment should be changed as well. A good example of this is as follows.

The Final Decree has specified that you are the noncustodial parent who may visit with her children every other weekend. During the last 6 months, your little boy has not adjusted well to the reduced time with you. He calls you every day crying. His grades in school have decreased and his teacher is aware of his yearning for you. Your discussions with the teacher indicate her willingness to testify that she believes the boy's performance in school has dropped due to the decreased time he has with you.

You have asked your former husband for increased time with your child.

He steadfastly refuses.

In the above scenario, certain circumstances have changed. The child was not demonstrating this type of reaction when you had more liberal visitation before. In this situation, a Judge might be quite willing to change the Final Judgment so that you and the boy would have more time together. Judges are motivated by law to do what is in the best interests of a child.

Generally, Judges do not like to modify a Final Judgment. However, when the circumstances change and the reasons for modifying a Final Decree are compelling, they are likely to do so.

ENFORCEMENT MOTIONS

In certain cases, a parent may have a liberal visitation schedule which is quite acceptable to that parent. The problem is that the other parent refuses to abide by the schedule.

In a split custody case, the noncustodial parent for the oldest child, refused to return the child to the primary residential parent at the end of each visitation period. Additionally, this interfering parent, who was the custodial parent for the other children, would often prevent the younger children from visiting with the other parent as well.

In cases such as this, one can schedule a Hearing to request that the Judge enforce the Final Decree.

In such cases, where the evidence is clear that the Final Judgment has not been carried out, the Judge will generally side with the injured party and order that the Final Judgment be enforced.

In some cases, this may work well. Unfortunately, *the parent who has been willing to violate a Final Decree, may also be quite willing to violate an Enforcement Order.*

Thus, even though one may have obtained a legal document that specifies that his or her visitation rights are to be enforced, this does not mean that the visitation will necessarily occur.

CONTEMPT MOTIONS

When a provision of a Final Judgment has been violated and it appears to be a deliberate violation, one may seek an Order from the Court finding the opposing side "In Contempt." Here, one is not only asking that the Final Judgment be enforced, one is also asking that the violator be punished.

The range of punishments can be as simple as the Judge finding the guilty spouse to be In Contempt, to other possibilities. Some of these include:

making the violating spouse pay the attorney fees for both attorneys;
threatening to put the violating spouse in jail;
threatening to remove the children from the primary residential home.

More extreme options include:

putting the violating spouse in jail;
moving the children from the violating spouse's custody to the custody of the nonresidential parent.

What typically happens?

Usually, the least threatening punishment is applied first. In other words, the violating spouse is found "In Contempt." Should there be repeated offenses, eventually the Judge might be compelled to use some of the more drastic punishments.

How often are the more drastic punishments applied?

Rarely.

THE ATTORNEY

Having now reviewed some of the major aspects of the judicial process, I will spend some time discussing the attorneys and their role. However, I will only briefly comment here because Chapter 19 will discuss the matter in considerable detail.

Attempts to settle the child visitation dispute successfully requires a good attorney. While attorneys differ considerably in their style and competency, their role in the visitation dispute is relatively clear.

The attorney's job is to represent you in the legal arena to the best of his or her ability. This includes many things.

Explaining the laws to you in a way that you can understand.

Outlining what your rights and options might be.

Handling issues from the opposing side.

And representing your case in the Courtroom.

What you tell your attorney is privileged information. In other words, your attorney cannot discuss anything unless you have given him or her permission to do so.

A good, honest, and open, working relationship with your attorney is essential in attempting to resolve a visitation dispute through the legal system.

THE ATTORNEYS' MOTIVES

What motivates attorneys?

While each attorney is subject to his or her own desires, dislikes, and biases, there are some general motivators which apply to most attorneys.

First, attorneys are motivated to help their clients.

It's their job.

However, I must tell you that most attorneys that I have dealt with seem to intrinsically feel a genuine desire to help their clients in the legal setting.

A second motivator for most attorneys is to have a good relationship with other attorneys. This only helps an attorney to be more successful in achieving results that help his or her clients. It also can be helpful to the attorney's financial status.

Attorneys operate generally on a "good ol' boy" system. Whether this is right or wrong could be a matter for debate. In any event, it doesn't really matter. The "good ol' boy" system is a reality and must be dealt with. More on this in Chapter 19.

Third, attorneys are motivated to have a good relationship with Judges and to make good appearances before them in the Courtroom. The reasons are similar to those listed in the paragraph above regarding attorneys' relationships with each other. There is one critical difference however.

The Judge makes the decisions.

It is best to keep that person happy.

As one attorney told me, when there is an election for a judgeship, a smart attorney makes a generous contribution to *both* candidates' campaigns.

Finally, most attorneys are motivated to make a good living. Many do. Some command fees as high as $400 or more per hour. By making their clients happy, having good relationships with fellow attorneys, and maintaining the respect of Judges, an attorney increases the likelihood that he or she will make a good living in the legal arena.

THE JUDGE

The Judge represents the laws of the state and the country.

It is the Judge's responsibility to make a decision about a dispute in light of the existing laws. To accomplish this, the Judge tries to stay as impartial as possible. The Judge guides the legal proceedings in as fair a manner as possible and then makes a decision.

Judges have tremendous discretion in making the decisions they do. When it comes to visitation disputes, often the picture is not as clear to the Judge as perhaps each combatant believes that it is. As such, two Judges hearing the same exact case might come up with different decisions.

THE JUDGE'S DECISIONS

Judges are human. Like attorneys and like ourselves, they are subject to their own set of motivators.

Judges want to be viewed as good.

Judges want to be viewed as fair.

Judges want to be viewed as doing what is right.

Most Judges are former practicing attorneys. They too, have relationships to consider beyond your case.

And they do.

When it comes to custody and visitation disputes, Judges often have their own biases.

Some Judges have gone on record as saying that they always give custody to the mother. Others claim to be more open-minded when it comes to the rights of fathers seeking custody.

In cases where a custodial parent is attempting to alienate a child against the nonresidential parent, one Judge may give a lengthy lecture in the Courtroom and find the alienating parent In Contempt. Another Judge hearing the same case, may provide a Court Order to force the alienating parent into therapy. Still another Judge might remove the child from the custodial parent and place him or her temporarily with the nonresidential parent. This is a good example of the discretion that Judges enjoy.

Part of what gives Judges such leeway in their decision making, is the principle, "reasonable men differ." Judges assume that they will differ with each other and that it is generally reasonable to expect differences. When a decision is shown to be unreasonable (given that "reasonable men differ"), then that decision can be overturned through an Appeal to a different Court (known as the Appellate Court).

Unfortunately, showing that a decision is unreasonable is not so easy to do.

For this reason, when a case is appealed, a very low percentage of cases are successful in their appeal. Judges prefer not to overturn another Judge's decision. Furthermore, if the prior Judge's decision appeared reasonable, even if the present Appellate Court Judge (the one who hears an Appeal) does not agree with the outcome, he or she is bound *not* to overturn it. Remember, to overturn a Judge's decision requires demonstration of a major error, such as the Judge acting in an unreasonable way.

There are good points and bad points for having this particular principle of "reasonable men differ."

The primary good point is that cases are not tried over and over again. The major bad point is that when a Judge makes a bad decision, it is a decision that we are likely to be stuck with.

As we all know, our personal lives can affect the way we operate in our profession. Judges are not exempt from this human characteristic.

A male Judge whose first wife did everything she could to alienate their children from him, may be less receptive to an angry mother in a custody battle. Similarly, a female Judge who has been personally hurt by someone who has the same appearance and mannerisms as the father in an ongoing visitation dispute, may be less than favorably receptive to this man's wishes.

A good attorney is knowledgeable of such biases among the Judges that he or she appears before. This knowledge might prove to be a critical factor in a visitation interference case.

BALANCING THE FACTORS

As we can see, the legal system has its different variables that must be dealt with in order to manage a visitation interference problem. To increase the probability of successfully resolving a visitation interference dispute through the legal system, many factors must be considered and attended to. Many pieces need to fall into place.

One must have patience.

One must choose the right attorney.

One must present the right evidence.

One must appear before the right Judge.

And so on.

═19═

HOW TO SELECT
AN ATTORNEY

Individuals combating an interfering parent need to be represented by a good attorney.

In this Chapter, I will outline a variety of issues that one should consider in trying to identify the right attorney to take on a visitation interference dispute. While there are no magical methods to guarantee proper selection, there are certain guidelines that one should follow to try to increase the likelihood of picking the right attorney.

I will try to describe these points in this Chapter.

RECOMMENDATIONS OF FRIENDS

How do most people select an attorney?

Typically, a friend recommends someone.

The friend says something like this, *"She is a great attorney"* or, *"He is a real sharp lawyer."* Information such as this can be helpful. However, to choose an attorney based on such limited information is not advised.

Law is a vast field and has many areas of specialization. In visitation interference, we are dealing with the "civil" area of the law as opposed to the "criminal" area of the law.

When someone is charged with murder, one is probably better off with a criminal attorney.

On the other hand, someone who specializes in defending accused murderers is probably not the best choice to represent someone who is being deprived of visitation with one's offspring.

Area of specialization is an important variable in choosing an attorney. The next section will spell this out in more detail.

SPECIALIZATION

As noted above, visitation disputes fall into the "civil" area of law. Within the civil area, there are many sub-areas. The major sub-area that we are interested in is know as, "domestic relations." Domestic relations provides the battleground known as "family law."

When an attorney finishes law school, that does *not* qualify the attorney to be a specialist in family law.

To obtain the status of a specialist, one must take a certain amount of post-law school education and pass a test to receive certification as a specialist in family law.* This is referred to as "Board Certification."

Individuals who are Board Certified in family law have documented their knowledge of the area.

Thus, when one is searching for an attorney to resolve a visitation dispute, a general rule of thumb is to see if one can identify an attorney who is Board Certified in family law. However, some States do not offer Board Certification in family law. Further, it is very important to note that there are many attorneys who are not Board Certified in family law who can handle a visitation dispute case rather well. In fact, I really should emphasize this point to you.

Some attorneys choose not to become Board Certified.

Board Certification by itself does not guarantee that the attorney is a good one for your case. Rather, all it guarantees is that the attorney has passed a number of requirements which documents knowledge of the family law area. There are attorneys who have the knowledge of family law and the expertise in family law, who simply choose not to document it by seeking Board Certification.

The most prestigious certification in family law is provided nationally by the American Academy of Matrimonial Lawyers (AAML).

This is important to keep in mind.

I have interacted with some attorneys who are not Board Certified in family law who handle divorce, custody, and visitation issues rather well. However, to the uninformed individual, these attorneys become harder to identify when they do not carry Board Certification in family law.

Thus, if one is trying to *rapidly* identify an expert in family law, it is easiest to start off with an attorney who has documented his or her knowledge of family law by becoming Board Certified. However, just because an attorney is Board Certified in family law does not guarantee that this is the right attorney for your case.

RATING THE ATTORNEY

Wouldn't it be nice if there was a rating system available on the attorneys in your town that you were considering to represent you?

There is.

In your local library, there is a set of books known as the "Martindale-Hubbell Law Directory" which provides such a rating system.

The Martindale-Hubbell volumes list most attorneys and provide ratings of them by other attorneys and members of the Judiciary. Let's discuss the "Legal Ability" ratings that are provided in Martindale-Hubble.

These ratings fall into one of three categories:

Rating	Legal Ability
A	"From very high to preeminent"
B	"From high to very high"
C	"From fair to high"

An "A" rating is awarded to less than 10% of attorneys.

A "B" rating is awarded to less than 25% of attorneys.

Notice how the ratings are in a range.

A "C" rated attorney could be one who is viewed as "high" in legal ability. A "C" rated attorney can also be one who is rated only as "fair." Further, a "C" rated attorney may be viewed by his or her peers as being somewhere between "fair" and "high" on legal ability. From the rating system, you and I have no way to know just where a particular attorney "lands" in that wide net of "fair" to "high."

Hence, the Martindale-Hubbell rating system is not perfect.

Nevertheless, the Martindale-Hubble legal ability rating provides one way to see how other attorneys view the attorney that you are considering.

An "A" rated attorney is highly regarded by his or her peers.
A "B" rated attorney is well rated by his or her peers.

Thus, when one is looking to quickly narrow down choices in selecting an attorney for a visitation interference problem, a good first step is to identify someone who is Board Certified in family law and who has an "A" rating in the Martindale-Hubbell volume.

Unfortunately, these two factors alone will not guarantee you a superior choice of attorney. Other factors must be considered as well.

EXPERIENCE

While an "A" rated, Board Certified family law attorney is quite likely to be a good attorney for working through a visitation dispute, a key factor to consider is the experience of the attorney in the specific area your case is in.

This is true whether the attorney chosen is Board Certified or not.

It is also true whether or not the attorney is "A" rated or "B" rated.

The ideal experience to look for, is an attorney who has seen hundreds of cases of visitation interference. It is even better if that experience was primarily obtained in the town that your case is in.

There are some family law attorneys who are "A" rated, yet do not deal with visitation disputes. For example, some may specialize in adoption. The attorney who is Board Certified in family law, is "A" rated in Martindale-Hubble, and specializes in adoption, is probably not going to be the best selection to represent you in a visitation dispute.

THE ADVANTAGES OF EXPERIENCE

Why is prior experience with visitation issues a key consideration in selecting an attorney?

There are several reasons.

First, the attorney who specializes in this area and who has seen hundreds of cases, knows what is likely to be accomplished and what is not likely to be accomplished. This can save you a significant amount of grief and money.

Second, if the attorney has seen many of these cases, he or she has a track record which you can find out about.

You can talk with other attorneys, paralegals, and Court reporters. You can check actual Court records of cases the attorney you are considering has been involved with. You can sit in on Hearings the attorney may be participating in.

These opportunities can give you an idea about the experience and success of such an attorney.

Third, the highly experienced attorney in visitation disputes is more likely to be efficient in handling the legal issues. If he or she has prepared hundreds of such Motions on visitation interference, it may only take him or her 15 minutes to do so. Someone with less experience may take over an hour.

Most attorneys charge by the clock.

Time is money.

Finally, the attorney highly experienced in visitation disputes has an advantage in knowing how to deal with you. He or she is likely to be very understanding yet very realistic in the advice given. Such an attorney will be more likely to know which areas to talk to you about and which areas not to waste time on. He or she is also likely to have numerous "tricks" up his or her sleeve for use in the Courtroom. The less experienced attorney may not have developed the special Courtroom techniques that a highly experienced attorney probably has.

In brief, we now have three criteria to consider in quickly identifying an appropriate attorney for representation in a visitation dispute:

1. Board Certification in family law;
2. "A" rating in Martindale-Hubbell;
3. Highly experienced in visitation dispute cases.

Now let me "throw in a monkey wrench."

Not every highly experienced, Board Certified, "A" rated family law attorney, is guaranteed to be a good choice to represent you.

Let's say such an individual is "burned out".

Or, say the individual acts like and looks like your former spouse.

Clearly, the three criteria I listed above are best used as guideposts and not as ironclad rules.

PROFESSIONAL RELATIONSHIPS

Professional relationships may play a key role in an attorney's effectiveness in a particular visitation dispute.

The attorney who gets on well with the Judge has somewhat of an edge over an attorney who has a bad relationship with a particular Judge. Similarly, an attorney who gets on well with the other party's attorney may be able to get more accomplished than two attorneys who do not get on well.

If attorney A and attorney B hate each other, they may use the dispute between you and your former spouse as an opportunity to wage their own personal warfare. On the one hand, this could lead to making your dispute with your former spouse more complicated and costly. On the other hand, the personal animosity might motivate your attorney to take a special interest in your case compared to others he or she may be working on.

Things are not always so clear.

As another example, assume attorney A and attorney B hate each other. Attorney B may be so sick of attorney A, that attorney B gives in, so that attorney B doesn't have to deal with attorney A.

In this case, you are the winner if you chose attorney A. But what if you had been stuck with attorney B?

See why professional relationships can be so important?

In some respects, Martindale-Hubbell gives us some idea about how a particular attorney keeps his or her professional relationships. Someone who receives an "A" rating is highly regarded by his or her peers. Thus, a good rating in Martindale-Hubbell is suggestive that the attorney has good relationships with his or her colleagues.

Unfortunately, this does not mean that the attorney has good relationships with every other attorney and with every Judge. As we noted above, some attorneys don't get on with each other. Further, some excellent attorneys don't do well in front of certain Judges.

These issues cannot be properly evaluated by Martindale-Hubbell.

The specific relationship that your attorney has with the opposite attorney and the specific relationship that your attorney has with the Judge in your case, need to be assessed on their own. You should specifically ask your attorney about these particular relationships.

The Board Certified attorney in family law who is "A" rated and specializes in visitation disputes, yet has a poor relationship with the Judge handling your case, is probably not the attorney you want to choose to represent you.

ATTORNEY STYLE

You need to have a good, open, honest, working relationship with your attorney. A good attorney will be patient with you but will not allow you to waste a lot of your time, or the attorney's time.

A good attorney will listen to what you have to say but not let you go on endlessly. He or she will keep you off of unnecessary topics.

The more you talk, the more you spend.

If you rant and rave emotionally for 45 minutes, you may feel better but you will have to pay for it. On the other hand, visitation interference disputes are emotional. You are not expected to be unfeeling.

The good attorney will know how to balance the time to allow you to cover the legal issues as well as handle some of the emotional concerns that come up.

The attorney who tells you whatever he or she thinks you want to hear is not providing you a good service. You are paying for expert advice, not for someone who wants to just make you feel good. While it is nice when you can have both, if one has to be chosen over the other, it is better to have good advice and not hear what you want to hear, as opposed to bad advice but hearing what you think you want to hear.

A good attorney keeps you out of Court as much as possible. Representation in the Courtroom is very expensive. Many clients find Court appearances to be very stressful.

Some attorneys find them stressful as well.

If your attorney can accomplish your goals outside of the Courtroom, you are more likely to benefit in the long run.

A good attorney will answer your phone calls. And he or she will do so within a day. You will not be ignored. However, the good attorney will not pamper you either.

The bottom line question when it comes to attorney style issues is this: "Do you feel comfortable working with this individual?"

If the answer is no, you probably need to find a different attorney.

FEES

Legal work is expensive. There are no two ways about it. However, the issues are not as straightforward as one would like.

Assume you have seen attorney Smith who has seen hundreds of visitation interference cases and she charges $300 per hour. Assume you have also met with attorney Jones who has seen few such cases and is willing to charge only a $250 per hour. On the face of it, it might seem that one is getting a bargain by choosing attorney Jones. It would appear that one could save $50 per hour. If twenty hours of legal work are involved, this suggests a potential savings of $1000.

Notice I said the word "potential." Because attorney Jones does not have the experience that Ms. Smith does, you may not accomplish what you have set out to do even if you are to save $1000. Further, you may not be saving $1000 if it takes attorney Jones three times as long to get the legal work done than it takes attorney Smith, who is highly experienced in these cases.

The issues get even more complex if you think of some of the other things I suggested you consider when choosing an attorney.

What is attorney Jones' relationship with this particular Judge like?

How does attorney Smith get on with your adversary's attorney?

As you can see, examining fees can be more complex than one would imagine.

THE FINAL SELECTION

With these factors in mind, it should be apparent to the reader by now, that choosing the right attorney typically requires some work.

I highly recommend that after doing the preliminary research, such as reading Martindale-Hubbell and identifying who is Board Certified, and so on, one should interview three prospective attorneys.

Many attorneys will meet with you for the first time without charging you. When you call to make an appointment, see if they do provide a free initial consultation.

Let the attorney know that you are shopping around. Ask him or her all the questions you can think of. Ask yourself if you can work with this person.

Finally, keep in mind that your decision is not cast in stone. If you chose an attorney and find that he or she is not living up to your expectations, terminate the relationship and find a new attorney.

Remember, it is estimated that there are approximately 800,000 attorneys in the United States.

There are always other options.

SECTION SEVEN

ADDITIONAL PARTICIPANTS

This Section will discuss those individuals who become involved in a visitation interference dispute, beyond the children and parents who are at the center of the conflict.

This Section is divided into three chapters.

In Chapter 20, I describe some of the motivations that often stimulate those who become involved in others' visitation disputes.

In Chapters 21 and 22, I discuss the various types of individuals who participate in the child visitation interference conflict.

20

THE MOTIVATIONS TO PARTICIPATE

The major contributor to a visitation interference situation is typically the custodial parent. However, in certain cases, other individuals may become involved in the visitation interference difficulty as well.

Some of these individuals may be closely involved with the custodial parent, such as friends and relatives. Others, such as teachers, guardians, and mental health professionals, may also become involved.

This Chapter will focus on some of the motivations that drive other individuals to participate in a visitation interference situation.

It should be noted that these motivations apply to both informal participants (for example, the best friend of the custodial parent) and professional participants (for example, the Guardian Ad Litem).

In this Chapter, I will review five major motivational types. I have labelled these as follows:

The Well Intentioned
The Power Seekers
The Chaos Creators
The Sadistic Meddlers
The Fearful Abandoners

Each type contributes to the visitation interference problem. Some may do so deliberately; others do so inadvertently.

Let's take a look at each of the different motivational types.

THE WELL INTENTIONED

Many individuals who contribute to a visitation interference situation enter it with very good intentions.

They believe they are helping the child involved.

They feel they are making a positive contribution to the situation.

They believe that they are on the "right" side.

Unfortunately, such individuals are often duped by the custodial parent or only partially informed as to what is actually occurring.

Friday after school, Gail goes to her best friend Beth's house to spend the weekend, as was arranged by Gail's mother. However, Gail was supposed to spend the weekend with her father. Beth's mother had no idea that this was the case. The father eventually found out where Gail was and came to the house to get her. Gail's mother, conveniently left town for the weekend. She "forgot" to leave a phone number in case of an emergency. Unable to reach Gail's mother, Beth's mother decided that she would not give Gail to her father. Beth's mother had previously been told horrible things about the father by Gail's mother. In order to "protect" Gail, Gail's father was ordered to leave the premises.

In this example, Beth's mother was not acting in a malicious manner. Rather, she was doing only what she thought was right. The girl's father had been presented as a bad man. No information was provided to verify that this particular weekend Gail was to spend with her father. Gail's mother was unavailable to discuss the situation. In this case, it is entirely understandable why Beth's mother took the position she did.

Such is the case with the well intentioned visitation interferer. The motivations are good but the actions contribute to the visitation interference difficulty.

THE POWER SEEKERS

Some individuals become involved in a visitation interference situation for an entirely different set of reasons. In this section, I will discuss the, "Power Seekers."

John is a volunteer Guardian. He completed High School but never lived up to his own aspirations to become a college educated professional. He likes to volunteer to work for organizations where he can enjoy feelings of authority. He secretly resents people who have been successful and has told others that *"... all attorneys are scum."* John had previously ran unsuccessfully for minor political office. John is the Guardian Ad Litem for 11 year old Harrison. Harrison's father is a successful architect. When Harrison's father complained to the Guardian that his ex-wife was interfering with visitation, his complaint fell upon deaf ears. However, when the ex-wife claimed to the Guardian that Harrison's father was rude to her when he would come to pick up Harrison, the Guardian arranged to be hiding in the house of the ex-wife when Harrison's father came. Harrison's father had no idea the Guardian was in the house. It didn't matter; the father acted in his typical calm manner. The next day, the attorney for Harrison's father received a fax from the Guardian, threatening to remove Harrison from his father's custody unless the father, *"... got himself under control."*

In this situation, a Court appointed professional has embroiled himself in a visitation interference situation and has unjustly taken sides.

Why?

Because of his own personal motivations to exert power.

The Guardian's actions in this case only served to strengthen Harrison's mother's resolve to interfere with visitation.

Custody and visitation disputes are a perfect opportunity for the power seeking individual to satisfy some personal motivation by exerting influence over "captured" individuals.

THE CHAOS CREATORS

The second motivational type to be discussed is the "Chaos Creator." Such individuals are quite different from the "Well Intentioned" participants to visitation interference.

The "Chaos Creator" likes to "stir things up."

The "Chaos Creator" gets bored easily.

The "Chaos Creator" likes to "see things happen."

These types of individuals can wreak havoc in a custody and visitation dispute.

Sue Ellen enjoyed stirring things up. She milked money from her best friend while encouraging this friend to split up with her husband. This eventually led her friend into an unwanted custody battle. She stirred up her friend's child, who had his own problems to begin with. Sue Ellen called the newspaper about another, quite bitter custody battle that was ongoing. Sue Ellen served as a "Team Mother" on her son's sports team and manipulated various team parents into conflict with each other. She volunteered at her son's school and turned people against a teacher's aide.

In this example, one woman rapidly engaged various parents and children into chaotic circumstances. Such is the world of the Chaos Creator.

These individuals seem to gravitate toward vulnerable people. Once a good "target" is identified, the "Chaos Creator" manipulates various situations the "target" has become involved in to make them more problematic.

Visitation interference situations provide a perfect "playground" for the Chaos Creator.

SADISTIC MEDDLERS

Some individuals like to hurt others. They seem to actually enjoy seeing people suffer.

Micki was an embittered woman who at one time had lost a custody battle of her own. She seemed to thrive on other people's pain. Her friends Jean and Corey owned an ice cream shop. During Micki's custody battle, Jean and Corey tried to stay involved, but neutral. Micki didn't like that. So she spread rumors that Jean was having an affair with Micki's divorcing husband. She enlisted other women to spread these rumors as well. Micki called the Health Department and reported that a large rat was seen running through Jean and Corey's ice cream shop. When Micki would see Jean and Corey's children, she would look at them with angry eyes.

She didn't stop with Jean and Corey. Her friend Marilyn was

hurting badly from her own divorce. Micki knew just what to say and do to bring out the pain in Marylin and her two children. Marylin began denying her husband Court Ordered visitation. Micki hurt many others along the way. Throughout her various escapades, when Micki was observed hurting someone, she would gloat to her confidants afterwards about her little "victory."

"Sadistic Meddlers" salivate at the opportunity to involve themselves in a custody and visitation battle. Everyone is a "fair target." Such individuals cause significant damage no matter what their role is in a visitation dispute.

The most dangerous "Sadistic Meddlers" are those who know how to cause pain without getting caught.

FEARFUL ABANDONERS

Some individuals find themselves contributing to a visitation interference situation because they are afraid of the consequences for *not* participating.

A custodial parent continually tried to interfere with a non-residential parent's attempts to visit with their mutual children at school. The custodial parent had gained a reputation for intimidating school personnel. When the noncustodial parent sought help from the school in resolving the problem, none was received, as there was significant fear about repercussions from the residential parent.

"Fearful abandoners" are typically passive participants to the visitation interference situation; they prefer to "not get involved." Unfortunately, this "uninvolvement" often facilitates the continuance of the visitation interference difficulty.

"Fearful abandoners" may be found not only in the schools but among friends, relatives and others.

MULTIPLE MOTIVATIONS

The five types of motivations that I have described above, do not cover all of the many possible situations. It is also important to point out that there are some individuals who have multiple personal motivations that facilitate contributing to various visitation interference situations.

Some "Sadistic Meddlers" also have "Chaos Creator" characteristics.

Some "Well Intentioned" individuals also have "Fearful Abandoner" tendencies.

Having discussed some of the motivations that others might have for participating in a visitation interference difficulty, let us now turn to where we are most likely to see these types of participants in visitation interference situations.

=21

COMMON PARTICIPANTS

Having reviewed some of the motivations that drive certain individuals (other than the custodial and noncustodial parents) to contribute to visitation interference, the reader will be better equipped to see how this unfolds in various situations.

For organizational purposes, this Chapter will focus on *common participants* in visitation interference situations. Chapter 22 will focus on *professional participants*.

TYPES OF COMMON PARTICIPANTS

Five major types of common participants will be discussed in this Chapter. These include:
  Relatives
  Friends
  Acquaintances
  Parents of other children
  New lovers
Each type can bring its own unique contribution to the visitation interference problem.

RELATIVES

When a couple divorces, the relationships between the divorcees and the relatives on each side typically change.

Aunt Mable who has never said a bad thing about your spouse, all of a sudden tells you what an awful person she has always thought your spouse to be.

Cousin Kenny questions whether you have actually made the right decision.

Your sister is ready to enlist her private detective brother-in-law to take your side.

Your father is saddened by the breakup.

Your mother is secretly delighted.

Naturally, your former spouse's relatives share their reactions with your former spouse as well.

Your ex- spouse's cousin has openly hated your guts from day one.

Your ex's brother is actually on your side, but afraid to say anything about it.

Your former mother-in-law would like to see the two of you back together again.

Your ex's father would like to see you dead.

Each divorce breeds different reactions among relatives on both sides. However, there is little doubt that changes in your relationships are very likely to occur.

Generally, you may become closer with members of your own family. Relatedly, you probably will become more distant with members of your ex's family. Of course, exceptions always occur. Nevertheless, when you get divorced, expect that you will most likely also become divorced from your ex's family as well.

If your divorce has escalated into a visitation interference situation, events may resemble those of the Hatfields and McCoys.

Your ex's brother threatens to, *"...punch your lights out."*

Your former mother-in-law tells your children that you are a, *"... no good, rotten, bum."*

Your sister offers to donate whatever money is necessary to, *"... nail that wicked witch to the Courthouse wall!"*

It probably doesn't stop there.

Your ex's sister is a "Sadistic Meddler"; she encourages your former spouse to not let you see the children.

Your cousin Bernie is a "Power Seeker"; he is pushing you into legal action that you really don't want to pursue.

At times, it might feel like everybody wants to "get in on the act":

You go to pick up your children at the designated visitation time at your former spouse's home. Your former father-in-law answers the doorbell and then curses you out. *"No way in Hell are you going to see those kids,"* you are told.

Get the picture?

Relatives take on all kinds of roles that can contribute to the visitation interference situation. Some relatives, particularly those of an angry divorced parent, are willing to take drastic action against the former spouse:

During a hotly contested legal battle over visitation rights, the parents of a custodial mother called the police and had the father arrested, claiming falsely that the noncustodial father threatened to kill them and to burn their house down.

In extreme situations, relatives of the former spouse may help the ex-spouse kidnap the children involved. As noted in Chapter 12, over 300,000 children are kidnapped by a family member.

FRIENDS

The multitude of reactions that friends have to divorce and visitation interference situations, can be similar to what is seen with relatives.

Your friends on the bowling team are equally divided.

Your former spouse's best friend describes you now as a, *"... deranged psycho"* whereas before you were revered as a, *"... kind and loving person."*

The couple next door refuses to talk to you or your ex-spouse.

Your friends' motives will vary as well. Some may be afraid that their own spouse will follow your former spouse's example. Others may be Chaos Creators. Others may take well intentioned yet interfering actions.

Joanne was the best friend of Pamela. Pam was just left by her husband. Joanne and Joanne's husband decided to take Pam's children away for a "vacation." The father had no idea where his children were. His attempts to get information about them were fruitless.

In this example, the father went through a round of unnecessary anguish. The children, may have been more in need of time with their father at that moment than on a "vacation" with non-family.

In another example:

Several female friends of a woman in a custody battle committed themselves to smear the divorcing husband's good name all over town. They repeatedly told the children involved that their father was a " (mentally) sick man" and encouraged the children to avoid being with him.

Convinced that they are doing right, friends like these interfere significantly in the ongoing relationship between the children and the nonresidential parent.

ACQUAINTANCES

When a divorce has deteriorated into a visitation interference situation, acquaintances of the divorcing couple may become major players in the visitation interference problem. When this happens, often it is a "Power Seeker," "Chaos Creator," or, "Sadistic Meddler" who has found a situation to "play in."

A father rings the doorbell at his divorcing spouse's home to pick up his children for visitation. He is greeted by a woman who he barely knows but who now seems to be intimately involved with his divorcing spouse. This woman informs him that his children are "elsewhere," will not divulge where they are, and then proceeds to curse him out.

In this example, a woman with a substance abuse history and psychiatric problems, who only recently became very friendly with the custodial mother, now gets to play an important role in the daily lives of someone else's children. In fact, she gets to wield more power with the children on a daily basis than the noncustodial father. As this woman attempts to damage the father's relationship with his children and interfere with their visitation, he is relegated to the role of an outcast.

Let's take another example:

> In an early phase of a custody battle, a noncustodial parent went to pick up the children at the primary residence, only to find a note from the custodial parent that the children were at the home of individuals that the family had only recently begun to interact with. When the noncustodial parent arrived, the owners of the home treated the parent like a convicted mass murderer. Participating in the custodial parent's war against the nonresidential parent, these individuals manipulated the children to be cold and distant toward the nonresidential parent.

Once again, we see how other individuals can involve themselves in a destructive way in the battles of a family they barely know.

There is little doubt that when a prior acquaintance becomes embroiled in a visitation interference situation, it creates another unexpected obstacle for the noncustodial parent.

PARENTS OF OTHER CHILDREN

Visitation interference situations are often encouraged by parents of other children. Naturally, they have their own motivations, which differ from case to case.

A mother who was petrified that her husband might leave

her, helped another woman in a custody battle keep the children away from their father.

In a different scenario:

> An angry custodial parent fueled a group of similarly angry custodial parents to plot ways to prevent the children from seeing the noncustodial parent.

In many situations, parents who have engaged in visitation interference seem eager to teach their methods to other parents who are going through a divorce.

> Samantha had lost custody of her son. She encouraged her friend Jillian to do everything she could to obstruct the relationship between Jillian's divorcing husband and his children.

In some situations, parents of other children can be incredibly helpful in coping with a visitation interference situation; in other cases, such parents can make difficult circumstances even more trying.

NEW LOVERS

New lovers usually provide mountains of support for individuals recovering from a hotly contested divorce. However, such individuals can fuel the fire in many ways.

The new lover is often seen as a threat to the former spouse. The father may fear that he is being replaced. The mother may worry the children will like her "replacement" better.

New lovers have similar concerns.

Some worry that they will not be accepted by the children involved. Others are concerned that the former spouse will try to poison the children against them.

Clearly, emotions such as these in the former spouse and/or the new lover can help fire up visitation interference situations.

> A man had been denied access to his children for over three

months. When he finally got them, his girlfriend at the time, tried to persuade him to prevent his children from seeing their mother.

Craig was a 10 year old child in a split custody case. When he would visit his noncustodial father, he would "spy" for his mother about information on his father. The father's lover reponded to this by encouraging the father to stop allowing the child to visit.

These examples illustrate how the new lover may contribute to visitation interference. What about when the children actually react negatively to the new lover?

Children who dislike their parent's new lover, often "fall right into the hands" of the other parent who is intent on interfering with visitation.

For example, the interfering parent is often on guard for any "opening" to further encourage the child to have negative feelings toward the new lover. When the child says something negative about the new lover, the interfering parent salivates at the opportunity. Occasional statements such as, *"I wouldn't want to go there either if I had to interact with that slob"* could encourage a child to actively participate in a visitation interference situation.

As we can see, child visitation interference can draw participants from many different areas of life. Friends. Relatives. People we barely know. Often it is difficult to predict who will become a "common participant" to inflame an already heated situation.

22

PROFESSIONAL PARTICIPANTS

By the time a visitation interference problem is in full swing, a variety of professionals most likely have become involved. Unfortunately, sometimes their involvement contributes to the visitation interference problem itself.

There are good plumbers and there are bad plumbers. There are good automobile mechanics and there are bad ones.

The same is true for attorneys.

And teachers.

And social workers.

In fact, this is probably true for professionals in all occupational categories.

As we've discussed before, individuals who contribute to visitation interference problems have various motivations. Some examples include the "Well Intentioned", the "Power Seekers", the "Chaos Creators", and the "Sadistic Meddlers."

This Chapter will discuss various professionals who contribute to visitation interference situations.

The reader should be aware that the majority of professionals who become involved in a particular family's divorce, do not contribute to a visitation interference problem. On the contrary, most are willing to give their time and effort to eliminate a visitation interference problem.

Unfortunately, each professional group can have it's "bad apples." Some have distorted personal motivations; others may just be incompetent.

For whatever reason that "bad apples" get involved, they may contribute significantly to the visitation interference difficulty.

TYPES OF PROFESSIONAL PARTICIPANTS

This Chapter will review various professional participants to a visitation interference problem. These include:
> The Guardian Ad Litem
> The Mental Health Professional
> The Teacher
> The School Administrator
> The Organized Activity Personnel
> The Police
> The Attorney
> The Judge

THE GUARDIAN AD LITEM

When a custody battle is ongoing, the mother and father involved have attorneys to represent their best interests. Sometimes it is necessary for someone to be appointed to specifically represent the children involved. In such cases, a Guardian Ad Litem is appointed.

The Guardian may be asked to engage in various activities. Sometimes, the Guardian is charged with conducting an investigation of the parties involved to recommend to the Judge which parent should become the primary residential parent. Such an investigation could involve the Guardian reviewing legal documents, school records, and medical information. Additionally, the Guardian may interview the parents, the grandparents, the friends of the family, the teachers, and any other individuals that the Guardian believes might prove helpful in the report to be prepared for the Judge.

A second activity that Guardians may engage in is to "protect" the children. If one parent has been accused of sexually abusing the child, the Judge may have imposed supervised visitation. In that circumstance, the Guardian may be the one to do the supervision.

In other actions on "behalf of the children" the Guardian may decide that the children may require psychiatric assistance. The Guardian may make such a recommendation to the Judge who may Court Order it, or the Guardian may try to work out the appropriate arrangements, with the consent of the parents involved.

As we can see, the Guardian may have a lot of power in a custody and visitation dispute situation.

The Guardian may walk into a school and demand to see confidential records of a child that he or she has been Court Ordered to represent.

The Guardian may appear at a mother's home without notice, and inspect the home to determine if proper conditions to care for the children are being provided.

Where do Guardians come from?

Guardians are either paid or are volunteers.

Attorneys are often appointed to be Guardians for children in a custody and/or visitation dispute. When this is done, such an individual is designated as "Attorney At Litem." In addition to attorneys, there are also some individuals who present themselves as "Professional Guardians." Both "Attorney Ad Litems" and "Professional Guardians" usually charge for the services that they render.

Volunteers are individuals from all walks of life. Typically, they have gone through various amounts of training in a Volunteer Guardian Program. The volunteer Guardian Ad Litem may range from a retired psychiatrist to an unemployed 35 year old female with a psychiatric history.

Given the powers assigned to a Guardian in a custody or visitation dispute, it is not uncommon to discover horror stories.

> A socially inappropriate, unemployed, abnormally obese woman, was appointed as a volunteer Guardian in a bitter custody battle between a well-to-do accountant and his wife. The wife embraced the socially inept Guardian into her network of female friends and her campaign against her divorcing husband. A lonely woman, she was easily duped by the befriending mother. The Guardian began to harass the accountant involved. On several occasions, she disrupted his schedule by demanding meetings with him at her whim. She demanded that he provide unnecessary copies of documents costing him hundreds of dollars. She created several thousands of dollars in legal expenses for him. She recommended that the children be placed with the mother.

The type of havoc that can be created by a poorly trained and/or unsupervised Guardian can be mind boggling.

One Guardian was told repeatedly by an intelligent 11 year old girl, that she wanted to live with the noncustodial parent. The Guardian deliberately withheld the child's wishes from the Judge.

One Guardian would take the child out of his classroom at school and upset him to the point of crying.

A Guardian with a psychiatric history, put false quotes in her report to the Judge, in order to sway the Judge against one of the parents in a custody battle.

An unfortunate aspect of having a Guardian Ad Litem, is that if a "bad apple" is appointed, his or her motives and actions may not become evident to the Court. In certain Guardian Ad Litem situations, no one is directly supervising an inexperienced and poorly trained individual. Sometimes, it begs the question, who is guarding the Guardian?

THE MENTAL HEALTH PROFESSIONAL

Mental health professionals are often called upon by the Court when a custody or visitation dispute cannot be readily resolved. Such appointments come typically with one of three basic service assignments:

Mediation
Evaluation
Therapy

Each of these activities may be conducted by a wide range of individuals. At times, a doctoral level mental health professional will be appointed, such as a clinical psychologist or a psychiatrist. In other cases, some of the masters level mental health professionals might be involved, such as the social worker or mental health counselor. Some battling couples may find themselves dealing with "professionals" with even less training and experience than that.

Whether the mental health professional has a Bachelor's degree or has a Doctorate, is minimally experienced or highly experienced, a "bad apple" can cause significant problems.

With this in mind, let us now review issues of mediation, evaluation, and therapy.

MEDIATION

The purpose of the mediator is to negotiate an agreement between the two parties.

John wants to visit with his daughter 50 percent of the time but Mary wants him to visit with the daughter only on alternating weekends. Rather than spend thousands of dollars on attorney's fees and Court costs, the mediator tries to negotiate a settlement of the visitation issue. If an agreement can be reached, the parties will have saved themselves from experiencing much grief and spending substantial sums of money.

Because of the advantages that mediation offers, there has been a steady increase in the use of professional mediators in divorce situations. Sometimes the mediator is Court appointed; other times, the attorneys attempt to find a neutral mediator. Many attorneys are now engaging in the practice of mediation.

Regardless of who is the mediator, unfortunately there are some individuals who become embroiled in a visitation interference situation that cannot profit from a mediation experience.

A custodial parent with a significant history of telephone visitation interference, attempted to manipulate the mediator to impose a "telephone schedule" so that the custodial parent would have an easier time interfering with the phone calls given knowledge of the schedule.

One person's demands of the ex-spouse were so unreasonable, that mediation was utterly impossible.

One mediator was delighted when the hostile and unyielding couple engaged in a cusody battle, did not return for a second mediation session.

There are times when a mediator can inadvertently contribute to a visitation interference problem.

The mediator is motivated to convince the parties to make an agreement. As such, certain mediators try to use whatever skills and tactics available to achieve a settlement.

A parent who is currently interfering with visitation, can sometimes keep the mediation sessions going for as long as possible without reaching an agreement.

For example, a parent suggests a mediation meeting every two weeks. During the sessions, no commitments are made. As months roll by, the visitation interference continues; no agreement has been reached. Such a manipulative parent may dangle the "promise" of visitation cooperation as the negotiations go on for months, only to abruptly terminate the mediation when it appears that the charade will no longer work.

What happens to the parent who has carried out such a devious plan? Nothing.

When a couple like this one is Court Ordered to mediation, the content of the mediation sessions is usually confidential and not reported to the Court. The only thing that is typically reported to the Court is the nature of an agreement, or the fact that the mediation has failed. Either party can terminate mediation at any time.

Thus, a Well Intentioned mediator could be easily manipulated by a calculating, visitation interfering parent.

A Court appointed mediator is successful only if an agreement is reached. Such mediators are paid for their positions. It would appear that the more successful the mediator is in reaching agreements, the more job security there may be. A mediator who cannot help couples reach agreements, is probably not needed.

With this type of underlying motivation, some mediators may "armstrong" a vulnerable parent to an agreement that the parent believes will actually contribute to a visitation interference difficulty.

For example, a visiting parent is experiencing visitation interference and the residential parent is trying to make an agreement that would allow the residential parent to relocate 40 miles away. The nonresidential parent is convinced that this tactic will only facilitate the interference with visitation. Intent on establishing an agreement, the mediator joins with the custodial parent to put heavy pressure on this issue. In such a situation, the naively trusting, dependent, or battle-weary parent may feel compelled to give in and make the agreement. In this situation, the mediator has unwittingly contributed to the visitation interference problem.

EVALUATION

Many Judges do not like to deal with custody and visitation disputes. In these situations, it is rare if not unheard of, for both parties to be pleased with the Judge's final decision. As such, some Judges like to have a mental health professional examine the situation and make a recommendation to the Court. From the Judge's perspective, there are many advantages to this.

First, few Judges will claim to have sufficient expertise in the psychological aspects of families and their disputes. By referring the family to a mental health professional for an evaluation, the Judge can argue that his or her decision was influenced by the independent mental health expert's recommendations.

Put more simply, a Judge can claim, "*... don't blame me - - the psychologist recommended it !*"

On the face of it, why would anyone think that there would be *disadvantages* for referring a custody or visitation dispute to a mental health professional? Unfortunately, there are many.

Before going into the disadvantages, let's talk a bit about the process of a mental health evaluation.

What exactly happens when one undergoes an evaluation by a mental health professional? This will depend very much on the individual who is conducting the evaluation of the family.

A social worker is likely to conduct a different evaluation than a psychologist or a psychiatrist. However, two psychologists may also conduct entirely different types of evaluations. The same is true for the other types of mental health professionals I have mentioned. Nevertheless, a typical scenario might be as follows.

A psychologist is appointed to do a family evaluation to make recommendations to the Judge for visitation and custody. The psychologist interviews both parents individually and together. Each child in the family is interviewed by the psychologist also individually and together. A variety of psychological tests are administered to each family member. School records are evaluated. Prior mental health records of each family member are examined as well. A handful of individuals who are close to the family from each side, be they grandparents, friends, or other individuals, are spoken with. The psychologist spends many hours reviewing all of the information, interpreting the data, developing conclusions, and specifying these things in a written report to the Judge. Specific recommendations for custody and visitation are provided. A significant amount of time, energy and dollars have been spent.

Unfortunately, the bottom line is this:
There is no scientific evidence available today that clearly determines who is likely to be the best custodial parent nor what is likely to be the best visitation arrangement in such a dispute.

As such, the mental health professional conducting the evaluation may seem to have almost as much discretion as a Judge may have in making a decision on visitation matters.

In a nutshell, *the mental health professional performing a custody or visitation evaluation, will be more influenced by his or her biases than by any scientific research.* Just as two Judges hearing the identical case can come up with different decisions about what to do, mental health professionals are in the same boat.

Despite the absence of scientific research to provide clear answers to visitation and custody issues, most evaluators try to do the best job they can within the scope of their limitations. Unfortunately, certain mental health professionals do not believe that they have any limitations in these issues. Some feel that they know best, based on their "experience."

This type of mental health professional is potentially dangerous.

Individuals like this do not inform the Judge, the attorneys, or the combating parents, about the lack of scientific evidence available on these issues. Instead, they allow the individuals involved to believe that the evaluator is fully armed with knowledge and facts to make a competent recommendation.

Because of the incompetence and biased behavior by certain mental health professionals in custody and visitation evaluations, I published a manuscript in 1993 in the *American Journal of Family Law* on this issue. As a psychologist myself, the incompetence and biases that I have seen among various mental health professionals who have immersed themselves in conducting custody and visitation evaluations is very disturbing. Such "professional" behavior can certainly contribute to worsening a visitation interference situation.

> A parent who had incessantly tried to alienate the children from the other parent, was ordered by a Judge to have a psychiatric evaluation. The mental health professional who conducted the evaluation informed the Judge that there was nothing wrong with the parent ordered to be evaluated. Within a short period of time, having been "cleared" by the mental health professional, the parent resumed the visitation interference and alienation strategies with more intensity and perseverance.

In this example, the mental health professional in the above case, made specific recommendations about the visitation schedule between the children and the divorced parents. Needless to say, the parent that he had stated was not disordered, subsequently failed to abide by the mental health professional's recommendations about visitation.

Without the benefit of sound scientific findings, mental health professionals are at risk to make serious errors in visitation and custody dispute evaluations.

THERAPY

The scientific literature on treatment of visitation and custody disputes is similar to that on evaluation of these disputes. Mainly, *there is no scientific evidence to suggest that mental health professionals can successfully treat a visitation interference problem.*

Despite the above, there are mental health professionals who believe that they know how to "treat" such situations. In addition there are some "bad apples" out there, who seem to thrive on these types of cases. Such individuals can cause significant difficulty for the parties involved.

In certain situations, the mental health professional may lose his or her sense of impartiality and become an advocate for one of the parties involved. Often this happens when one of the parents has gone to therapy during the divorce or post-divorce period. The greedy or power seeking mental health professional may contribute to an already belligerent situation.

A manipulative woman in a custody battle went for counseling with a social worker who was in practice with the woman's best friend's husband. The social worker not only began to see this woman in therapy, he had her bring in her various children for "family therapy" as well. All of this was done without the father's knowledge or permission. Having already demonstrated his biases, the social worker tried to get the father to come in for therapy with him. In Court, he testified on behalf of the mother (who had already established a visitation interference pattern) and suggested to the Judge that he, the social worker, should evaluate the entire family for a custody recommendation. As the father refused to participate in a biased situation like this, the social worker recommended to the Judge that the mother should have custody of all of the children. When the custody battle ended, the social worker sent the father a bill for over $2000 for his "work."

It should be noted what happened after the mother had been "treated" by this social worker. Two years following this social worker's involvement, the custodial mother refused to allow the father to visit with the children at all

THE TEACHER

Generally speaking, teachers are not likely to perpetuate visitation interference. Most believe in the importance of parent involvement and are happy to interact with interested parents regarding their children. Visitation interference by teachers generally occurs in one of two scenarios.

The first scenario involves the teacher following orders from higher level school officials.

The second involves deliberate actions by a "bad apple."

A teacher was ordered by a school board official not to interact with a child's nonresidential parent until claims by the custodial parent about legal papers being "drawn up" could be verified. The noncustodial parent was not aware of the situation. When the parent being restricted called to find out about the child's math test performance, the teacher refused to speak with that parent.

In this example, the teacher was not adopting a deliberate visitation interference strategy. Rather, the teacher was ordered not to interact with this particular parent. Unbeknownst to the teacher and the school board administrator, there was no truthfulness to the custodial parent's claim that legal papers were being "drawn up" to prevent the other parent's participation in the child's school life. This maneuver, known as the, "legal threat" technique was discussed in Chapter 6.

From time to time, a teacher becomes embroiled in a visitation interference situation by his or her own design.

A teacher was befriended by a manipulative residential parent whose daughter was in the teacher's class. This divorced parent had a significant track record of visitation interference. The residential parent convinced the teacher that the noncustodial parent was "evil" despite there being no basis for this accusation. When the noncustodial parent would attempt to have lunch with the child, the teacher would either call the child's residential parent or have an assistant principal come to the classroom to help prevent the nonresidential parent from seeing the child.

At times, a teacher may take action against a parent without being instructed to do so.

One teacher refused to return the telephone calls of a parent in a visitation interference dispute.

Some teachers don't want to deal with a bitter divorce situation. Such individuals may try to avoid the parents involved whenever possible.

Other teachers have personal reasons that lead them to become involved in the visitation interference conflicts of others. Perhaps they have had a negative relationship with someone similar in the past. Perhaps they just don't like this particular parent.

In either case, teachers can directly and indirectly influence a visitation interference problem.

SCHOOL ADMINISTRATOR

Most school administrators are motivated to avoid participating in a visitation interference situation. Unfortunately, there are some school administrators who may contribute to a visitation interference problem.

An angry divorcing residential parent was a volunteer at an Elementary School. This parent interfered whenever possible with the nonresidential parent's attempts for lunchtime visitation with the child. The nonresidential parent approached the Principal for help with the problem. The Principal would not return this parent's phone calls or letters. After a month of avoiding the noncustodial parent, the Principal finally informed this parent that she would have nothing to do with the resolution of the problem.

In another example:

A father had been trying to visit with his child at a Middle School but the custodial parent had made it very clear to the Principal that she did not want the child to see her father. The father provided Court documents to the Principal demonstrating his right of access to his daughter. The father lived 90 miles away from the child's school. Despite the Court orders, the school Principal told the father that he had to *"deal with the local parent"* and therefore would not cooperate in permitting the father to see his child at the school.

In this situation, the Principal indicated that he was *"extremely familiar"* with these types of situations in his *"twenty-eight years of experience."* Unable to afford continued legal action, the father was not permitted to exercise his legal rights to visit with his daughter at school.

ORGANIZED ACTIVITY PERSONNEL

At times, visitation interference may reveal itself in unexpected ways.

An angry divorced parent demanded that the child's soccer coach "under no circumstances" was to give the team schedule to the child's other parent.

In this instance, the soccer coach was placed in a no-win situation.

If he didn't comply with the custodial parent's demands, he was likely to face the wrath of this parent and potentially have a revolution by other parents of children on the team. On the other hand, if he didn't provide the schedule to the other parent who requested it, this could reflect negatively on the soccer league that the coach was representing; it also may have violated the coach's own standards of personal conduct.

In situations like this, whether it is the karate instructor, the gymnastics teacher, or the girl scout troop leader, there are individuals who will comply with the demand to interfere with visitation and there are those who will not.

Predicting who will and who won't participate is not always easy.

The highly skilled manipulative parent who is committed to visitation interference, finds that who the specific individuals are that become participants in the interference, really doesn't matter; sooner or later, unwitting accomplices will be found.

In this way, the parent who is successful in a visitation denial campaign can create a community-wide network of "co-conspirators."

THE POLICE

The police prefer not to get involved in "domestic disputes." It is understandable.

When a bank is being robbed, the police know that there are likely to be weapons involved and that injuries may occur. The goal is to catch the criminal without anyone getting hurt.

The police are well prepared.

When a divorced couple are fighting over visitation and the police are called, they are less likely to be shot at. However, sometimes somebody pulls out a concealed weapon and trouble begins.

In cases where weapons are not involved, there is another difficulty for police providing assistance in visitation disputes: at least one party is likely to be upset with the police officer.

In certain counties, if you have appropriate Court papers to document your right to visit with the child, the police will accompany you to the other parent's home and attempt to enforce the visitation. Unfortunately, there are two major problems with this.

First, most Court Orders are too vague for the police officer to be convinced that it is necessarily your turn for visitation. Court papers rarely specify the exact date that visitation transfers are to take place. When the terms "every other weekend" or "reasonable visitation" are used, the police officer rightly feels unable to enforce the decree.

Another major difficulty occurs when the child involved has been alienated by the custodial parent. Knowing that the custodial parent will be upset if the child demonstrates desire to be with the other parent, when the police officer arrives, the child states that he or she does not want to see the noncustodial parent. Most police officers will not take the child from a custodial parent if the child states that he or she does not want to go.

Again, while appearing to "protect" the child, visitation interference is encouraged.

THE ATTORNEY

A woman had just lost custody of her son after a bitter and lengthy custody battle. She fired her second attorney and informed her new attorney that her ex-husband had been sexually abusing the boy. From the attorney's office, she called the appropriate state agency and complained that her ex-husband was sexually abusing the boy in question. In the presence of the attorney, the woman told the investigator, *"Judge Eves didn't give me what I want, so now you will."*

In this example, the attorney's role in contributing to the visitation interference situation was set up by the client's complaint. The attorney did not know whether the allegation was true or not (although the woman's statement about the Judge made the State official on the telephone highly suspicious). Nevertheless, when such an allegation is made, the attorney is duty bound to protect not only the client but also the child involved. The fact that the abuse allegation was false, did not deter the attorney from encouraging the client to notify state officials.

Attorneys typically play an indirect role in fostering visitation interference. In a custody or visitation dispute, the attorneys represent the private armies of the two generals involved: the combating parents. As in the above example, the attorney may encourage the client to call state officials. Another attorney might take a different tack.

The attorney may set up an "Emergency Hearing" and file a Motion for a Restraining Order. As we discussed in Chapter 11, the Judge is now presented with the choice of leaving the child in the hands of an alleged sexual abuser or not. The Judge knows that allegation does not equal to proven guilt, but nonetheless must "protect" the child.

Such a situation is an example of how an attorney helps to interfere with the ongoing relationship with the parent and child.

Occasionally, one may encounter a self-serving attorney who gives advice based on what is good for the attorney and not for the parties involved. The advice given by such a "bad apple," may contribute to visitation interference.

> An angry parent in a split custody case complained repeatedly to an attorney that the former spouse refused to follow visitation guidelines. After repeated efforts in Court to solve the situation failed, the attorney advised the client to retaliate by interfering with the other parent's visitation schedule.

In another example:

> A custodial parent spent thousands of dollars in legal fees trying get the former spouse to cooperate with the visitation schedule. As the custodial parent's finances began to exhaust, the attorney advised the parent that the visitation problem could be solved by moving to another state and forgetting about the child.

There are many excellent attorneys who are competent and ethical in their practices. However, when a "bad apple" becomes involved, a visitation interference situation may deteriorate further.

THE JUDGE

Like attorneys, Judges do not seek to interfere with visitation. Most believe that it is important for the child to have access to both parents, and that these relationships should be encouraged.

Judges contribute to visitation interference when it is justified. The justification may not be correct; nevertheless, the Judge will do what he or she must do based on the evidence.

The father who is sexually abusing his child should have his visitation "interfered with."

The mother who is physically abusing her child should have her visitation "interfered with."

The child must be protected.

Unfortunately, when a false allegation of abuse is made, a Judge might contribute to the visitation interference situation by acting under the principle of "protecting the child."

No Judge seeks to disturb the relationship between a parent and child if it is not merited. By the same token, when a parent is shown to be interfering with visitation, often the Judge's "hands are tied."

If the Judge takes money away from the custodial parent, this could potentially hurt the child.

If the Judge puts the custodial parent in jail, this could potentially hurt the child.

Thus, Judges are often "forced" to contribute to a visitation interference situation, even when they do not intend to.

Judges. Attorneys. Guardians. Therapists. Teachers. Professions that typically help members of society. As we have seen, one "bad apple" can significantly contribute to worsening a visitation denial problem.

SECTION EIGHT

COPING WITH VISITATION INTERFERENCE

The parent dealing with a visitation interference situation, suffers a unique tragedy.

His or her child is alive but not accessible. He or she has not done anything wrong but is punished anyway. A treasured part of a parent and child's life is stolen, without adequate retribution. Attempts to resolve the problem often result in more punishment and pain.

In this Section, we will begin to address how to deal with a visitation interference difficulty.

Chapter 23 discusses issues involved in coping with the emotions often aroused by visitation interference.

Chapter 24 provides recommendations on how to deal with the children involved in these unfortunate situations.

Chapter 25 reviews how to deal with others who become embroiled in a visitation interference difficulty.

Chapters 26 and 27 discuss how to manage specific visitation interference methods.

=23=

MANAGING EMOTIONS

In this Chapter, I will try to address some of the emotional issues that arise when trying to cope with a visitation interference problem.

I must tell you, it saddens me that such situations exist and that there is no scientific evidence available as to how to best manage them. Nevertheless, I will try to give the best advice that I can, given my experience and awareness of relevant professional literature.

COMBATING SADNESS

I have yet to meet a parent suffering from visitation interference who did not also experience sadness. For those who view their children as their most treasured possession, to be stripped of important childhood time with them is a pain that can resist healing.

Unfortunately, often the efforts made to resolve the visitation interference situation only result in more pain.

Phone calls are prevented.

School visitation is disallowed.

Letters never arrive.

In certain cases, each effort to contact the child results in failure.

And more pain.

Parents who become targeted for a Parental Alienation Syndrome receive an even more unique experience. For those who experience it, it may be the shock of a lifetime.

The daughter who loved you dearly is now falsely claiming you have abused her.

The son who cherished his moments with you is now falsely accusing you of being a drug addict, liar, and cheat.

The child that savored every moment with you now curses you in public.

The innocence of childhood has been stripped away and you have become the target of it.

How can these situations not cause some degree of sadness?

Coping with the loss of a loving and open relationship with one's child is no easy task for the parent who has treasured that relationship. Nevertheless, unless the parent musters strength and perseverance in coping with this, he or she could end up in serious trouble.

Some parents become deeply depressed and require psychiatric hospitalization. Others attempt to kill themselves. Some attempt to kill the ex-spouse who is preventing appropriate visitation. Others resort to kidnapping. In some cases, attorneys and Judges have been attacked.

The parent who truly cares about one's children, will care about oneself: he or she will not allow such deterioration to occur. That parent will take the necessary steps to combat the sadness that could lead to terrible consequences if unchecked.

Is it appropriate for the parent who is suffering from visitation interference to have deep sadness?

Of course.

But you should not let it overtake you.

The first step in coping is to recognize that you have a problem beyond the visitation interference situation. The problem is that you hurt. You are sad. Maybe even depressed. Admit it. There is nothing wrong with admitting it. In fact, it is important that you admit it to yourself.

If you don't admit that you have a problem, then it becomes very difficult to directly address the problem. I can assure you, a problem like this will not just go away. To deal with it well, you must first admit having the problem.

Here's how you can judge if you are depressed:

Are you crying often?
Are you having trouble sleeping?
Are you having difficulty functioning at work?
Are you letting your home deteriorate?
Are you not enjoying things anymore?

Are you having problems with your appetite?
Are you losing weight?
Are you feeling hopeless and helpless?
Are you feeling like you would like to end it all?

Affirmative answers represent symptoms of depression. If you are experiencing them, you should attend to them.

Once the problem is recognized, one can start thinking about the types of things one must do to combat the problem. Some people are able to fight sadness and depression successfully on their own. Others cannot.

In some cases, professional help will be needed.

One should not be ashamed about getting professional help. In fact, if you need a professional to help you, you owe it to yourself and to your children to get it. I will discuss treatment issues involving mental health professionals later on.

Whether or not you require professional help, it seems to me that to successfully combat sadness and depression associated with visitation interference, one must develop a special way of thinking about the problem with your offspring. I call this the "right attitude."

Having the "right attitude" can be a potent weapon in fighting the negative emotions that come when one is denied access to one's child. Because of it's importance, I have reserved a special section of this Chapter to discuss the "right attitude."

Let's first discuss some other destructive emotions that can arise in a visitation interference situation.

CONTROLLING ANGER

A parent experiencing a serious visitation interference problem cannot help but experience anger as well.

Imagine the following.

You tried to make the divorce process as smooth as possible for your children, but your ex-spouse prevented it. Every effort you made to spare the children from the pain of separation was thwarted by your former spouse. You tried to do what was right but it didn't work. You went to the Courts. Time after time after time. Your attorney gave her best effort. The Judge seemed like a reasonable person. But they could not control your ex-spouse. At first you were denied various visitation opportunities and then your ex-spouse really cranked up the alienation attempts. Once it became apparent that the judicial system was powerless, your ex-spouse really went into high gear. Your children are alienated against you, unrightly so. Your relationship with your children appears lost. You are financially strapped. Every effort to do what is right has backfired in your face.

In this situation, who wouldn't be angry?
Angry at your ex.
Angry at your ex's attorney.
Angry at your own attorney.
Angry at the Judge.
Angry at former "friends."
Angry at the school Principal.
Yes, perhaps even angry with your children.
And yourself.

Unfortunately, anger can be a very destructive emotion. It can not only rip you up inside, it can lead you to hurt others. There is even some scientific evidence now to suggest that in certain cases, there may be an association between anger and cancer; there may also be an association between anger and cardiovascular disease (heart attacks and strokes are cardiovascular in nature).

Should the person who has gone through the scenario described above be angry?

Of course.

Should the person succumb to the anger and follow the destructive lead it suggests?

Of course not.

To successfully cope with the anger aroused by a serious visitation interference problem, one must learn to redirect the anger in a way that will make it more manageable.

Where the anger is intense, one must learn to reduce it.

Where the anger leads one to think about performing destructive acts, one must abandon it.

Wherever possible, if one can find a way to channel the anger into appropriate places, then one might stand a better chance of coping with it.

Having the "right attitude" is critical. Receiving appropriate professional help may be necessary. More on this in just a moment.

RETALIATORY URGES

Jill has lost custody of her two sons to her former spouse, whom she despises. She has pursued him through the Courts for years, but to no avail. She feels estranged from her children and blames her ex-husband. She would like to hurt him badly.

Parents who find themselves in Jill's shoes may often feel urges to "get even."

They may think about kidnaping the children.

They may think about murdering their former spouse.

Some would prefer to torture the other parent, feeling that death would be too easy.

Feeling urges to retaliate are normal. Acting upon them in such ways is not acceptable in our society.

What punishment would properly fit the crime of estranging a parent and child?

A hanging?

Death by injection?

Slow deliberate torture?

A $100,000 fine?

The answer is this:

There is no appropriate punishment to fit the crime of stealing the years of childhood from an ongoing relationship between a parent and child.

As such, one should recognize that retaliation urges can be dangerous. Killing your ex-spouse would devastate your children. It might even lead to *your* death (depending on which State you committed such a crime in).

When considering any type of retaliation, one must answer the following two questions:

Will this hurt your child?
Will this hurt you?

If the answer is yes to either of these questions, then the retaliation you have in mind is probably better kept as a fantasy.

The best approach to retaliation is to not become blinded by its urge.

That does not mean abandoning one's rightful anger at the other parent. It only means being "smart" about it.

Being smart about it, requires the "right attitude."

Let's discuss it.

THE RIGHT ATTITUDE

Sadness.
Anger.
Depression.
Hate.
Revenge.

These are common feelings among victims of visitation interference. Unfortunately, these emotions can lead you to actions that could boomerang in your face.

Such emotions need to be channelled properly.

Such emotions need to be utilized in the right direction.

The key here is to develop the "right attitude."

Let me explain.

There are times in life when no matter what you do you cannot turn a problem around. If your former spouse has out-maneuvered you and accomplished all of the terrible things against you that I have been discussing in this book, what are your choices?

At first blush ... not many good ones.

When you are in such a situation, where whatever you do does not help the matter, you feel stuck. The major option you have left is to decide whether or not you want this situation to eat you alive. A parent who loves one's children and has been estranged from them, could literally anguish oneself to death. But is this in the child's best interest? Is this in the parent's best interest?

I don't think so.

You need to understand that the love deep inside that your children have for you, will last beyond your own life. At the present time, the relationship between you is not good. But does that mean it has to be that way in five years? Ten years? Twenty years? Forty years?

No it doesn't.

The child who has been cut off from a loving parent never forgets that parent. Let me repeat: The child who has been cut off from a loving parent never forgets that parent. And sooner or later, that child will seek out that parent. There may be a lot of damage to overcome but nevertheless, the child will seek out the parent. Let me give you an example.

Roger's former wife did everything she could to alienate their daughter from him. As she was growing up, the mother appeared to succeed in this endeavor. However, when the daughter moved into her twenties, she began to piece together what her mother had done to her. Needless to say, Roger's daughter deeply resents what her mother had done to her. Today, the daughter shares a wonderful relationship with her father.

And so it is with Roger and his daughter.

Now, how about you?

A key part of the right attitude is understanding what has happened to you and your offspring and to have confidence that time is on your side.

The loving parent who has been estranged from his or her offspring should know that deep inside that child yearns for you. Sooner or later, that child will grow to ask questions. Sooner or later, the child will put the pieces together and will understand what the custodial parent has done. That child will most likely have deep resentment of the parent who denied that child years of childhood with the estranged parent.

So the first components of the right attitude are to:

Understand what the situation is
Have faith in your relationship with your child
Have patience
Control your retaliatory urges

Not let the situation eat you alive
Take good care of yourself

All of these are critical in keeping the right attitude. They make the present situation more tolerable. By themselves however, it is not enough. An important element must be added:

One must develop a "master plan."

THE MASTER PLAN

The major goal of the master plan is this:

When all is said and done, you and your child will have an enjoyable, fulfilling, and mutually rewarding relationship.

The issue then becomes, how do you get there? While every case is different, there are certain things to keep in mind.

The relationship you have with a child at age 8 could not possibly be the same as the relationship you have with that same child when he or she is no longer a child. In other words, your relationship with your offspring at ages 5, 15, 25, 35, and 55 will be different.

If you were estranged from your child at age 10, why can't you redevelop it later?

If you can't recapture the childhood years, why can't you enjoy the young adult or mid-adult years of your offspring?

Or even the later years of your offspring?

I am a very lucky man to live on the gulf coast of Florida. In this neck of the woods, many residents are retired. And many have interesting stories to share. There are parents in their 80's who have wonderful relationships with their children who are in their 60's. There are parents who had difficult relationships with their children in their twenties who became very close when the children reached middle age.

See the point?

If you keep your arms open, eventually, the estranged child will be able to come back to you. How you deal with it through all this time will be critical.

Thus, the first step in working on the master plan is to accept the fact that you are always the parent of that child. This will never change. *No matter how old you are, you will always be that child's parent.*

Always remember that.

Your child will eventually yearn to have your love and become strong enough to seek it.

You can take comfort in that.

The second part of the master plan is to figure out ways to make it easier for your child to come to you when he or she is able to do so.

Keep the doors open as best as you can. If your interactions are limited:

Do not guilt-trip your child.

Do not punish your child.

Do not be angry with your child.

He or she is only trying to survive. The child belongs to you but cannot express it directly.

Be understanding.

Be patient.

Be warm and accepting.

Keep those doors open!

Such an approach is very difficult, especially for a parent whose child has been alienated against him or her. When such a child curses at you, ignores you, disobeys you ... keep in mind that it may not really be directed at you. Understand what the child has been forced to do. Reassure the child that you love him or her. Don't get angry. Try not to take it personally.

I know that is very difficult, but try anyway.

Part of this strategy involves keeping whatever connections with the child you can.

If you can only speak on the phone, do so.

If you can only see the child on school grounds, do so.

If your only avenue is to be seen by the child on his or her way somewhere, then go ahead and be seen.

Make sure that the child knows that you have not given up on him or her. Make sure that the child knows that you are still interested in him or her.

No matter what the approach, keep the connection there.

For all you know, the child who is screaming and cursing you may be thinking deep inside, "*I love you..... I want you..... Please help me..... Please don't leave me....*" Keep this in mind.

If you have been a loving and giving parent all of these years, have faith in the inner workings of your child.

Finally, part of the master plan is to take all of the negative aspects and try to develop something positive out of it. My father always taught me, *"If you can turn garbage into gold then you have really done something."* This is part of your task.

Take your anger and use it to develop a good strategy for keeping the connection with your child. Utilize your urges for retaliation to become the best parent you can be when the opportunities for interacting with your child present themselves. Have faith that time is on your side.

Many parents who experience visitation interference have no idea that other parents have gone through similar experiences. Write your experiences down for others to profit from. Or join a support group; give as well as receive. Or educate your local politicians about what you are experiencing. Or volunteer to be a role model for a disadvantaged youth.

The bottom line is that you need to try to turn "garbage into gold."

If you can turn these negative experiences and feelings into something positive and constructive, then you have really provided the best possible retaliation.

SUPPORT GROUPS

Some individuals find it very helpful to join an appropriate support group. I encourage you to check into it.

You will find some groups to be helpful. Others will not be. Each person is different. So is each group. Not everyone can benefit from a support group. But you will never know unless you do some investigating.

There are many different types of support groups available.

Women's groups.

Men's groups.

Divorced parents groups.

Groups for mothers who are noncustodial parents.

Groups for fathers and grandparents.

Children's groups.

There is no shortage of support groups. The right support group can make a world of difference.

PROFESSIONAL HELP

Some individuals will need professional help. If you have the slightest concern that you might need professional help, I suggest that you seek it out.

If you seek professional help and find that it is not helpful, you could always terminate it.

If you don't seek professional help, then you will never know if the help indeed could aid you to feel better.

Keep in mind that the field of mental health, as I noted in Chapter 22, has significant limitations. Just because someone has earned a Doctorate, does not mean that that person can be helpful to you. Even more troublesome, is that a "bad apple" mental health professional may be convinced that he or she *can* help you (or act *like* he or she can help you) when in fact, he or she really can't.

How effective is therapy?

It really depends on the problem, the specific treatment that is applied, and the person applying it. Some professionals believe that the scientific literature suggests that when undergoing therapy, one-third gets better, one-third stays the same, and one-third gets worse.

From my own experience, all I can tell you is that a good therapist can make a world of difference. A bad therapist can make things much worse.

What about medications? There happens to be good scientific evidence for the effectiveness of certain antidepressant medications with certain types of depression.

The good news is that if a depressed person is put on the right medicine at the right dosage, significant improvement should occur within just a few weeks. Notice, however, that I said the *right* dosage and the *right* medicine. If you are put on an inadequate dosage or are on the medicine for an insufficient amount of time, it will not work properly. Further, if you do not follow your doctor's directions, it is unlikely that the medicine will be helpful.

The same is true for anxiety relieving medications. If properly used, they can be very helpful.

Whether one seeks therapy or medication to assist in coping with a visitation interference problem, the key is to try it and to evaluate its usefulness yourself. If you notice a positive difference, continue with it. If you see no changes or experience negative things, discuss it with your doctor. In some cases, you may need to find a different professional to help you.

How does one go about finding a good mental health professional in your area? Many of the rules about finding the right attorney that I laid out in Chapter 19 apply.

Find someone who is licensed to practice in the state that you reside in.

Find out what kind of experience that person has had in dealing with visitation interference problems.

Ask others about the professional.

See who your family doctor would recommend.

Check with a religious leader you have faith in.

See if you like the person recommended.

Finally, remember that your decision to see a particular professional is not cast in stone.

ROYAL MANNERS

If you follow all of the steps I have outlined so far in this book, I am confident you will be dealing better with the visitation interference problem facing you. However, there is one last strategy that could prove to be extremely helpful to you, if you are not following it already.

In all of your dealings with your children, your former mate, the attorneys, the Judge, the school teachers, the mental health professionals, relatives, friends, and so on: try to behave with *royal manners*.

I am advising you to be as noble, gallant, cooperative, giving, innocent, and reasonable as possible. Try to be the best example you can be. Give them *royal manners*.

Why do I say this?

The answer is simple.

The more you try to hurt others, lie, cause difficulties, argue, curse, scream, demand, and so on, the less help you will in sum receive. It will eventually backfire with an attorney, a Judge, and most importantly, your children.

Who gets angry at the benevolent Queen?

Who refuses to assist a charming Prince?

There are many advantages to taking the "High Road."

Adopt *royal manners*.

=24

DEALING WITH
THE CHILDREN

The parent embroiled in a visitation interference situation suffers a special pain.

So does the child.

In this Chapter, I will outline a variety of strategies that a parent might adopt when confronting a visitation interference problem. While every case is different and all possibilities cannot be addressed in this Chapter, I believe the reader will find the general strategies I have outlined here to be quite useful.

SHOWING LOVE

The child who is the center of a visitation interference dispute bears a special burden. All children need love; this child needs it even more.

The child who has been alienated from a parent suffers a special loss.

Whether we like it or not, we inherit the genes of both of our parents. Each of us has a part of us that is our mother, and another part that is our father, embroidered into one. If prior to the separation, the child had a loving relationship with the currently alienated parent, that child's loss is even deeper. *To be forced to act in an antagonistic way toward a parent that is loved, is a cruel experience.* Such a child can only benefit from the understanding and warmth of the estranged parent.

The parent who is unable to see his or her child might ask, *"How can I show my love to my child if I cannot even get to see my child?"* In later sections of this Chapter, I will provide practical information about how to convey love in such a situation. For those who do have the opportunity to interact with their child, utilize every opportunity.

There are many things that one can do to show a child that he or she is loved. Of course, one must always consider the age of the child, the sex of the child and the specific relationship between the parent and the child. Take the suggestions that are provided here and adapt them to your unique situation.

No child is too young or too old to be told by their parent, *"I love you."* If you have been the type who has normally not uttered those words to your child, learn to do so. Introduce the phrase, *"I love you,"* into your interactions gradually and then slowly increase the frequency of it.

Tell your child when you say goodbye.

Tell your child when he or she has done something that makes you proud.

Tell your child when he or she has done something to make you laugh together.

Whenever the moment appears right, tell your child, *"I love you."*

For those who feel "stiff" in uttering these critical words, occasionally add the child's name. *"I love you, John." "Mary, I love you."* Personalize it in other ways as well. *"I love you, son."* Or, *"I love you, sweetheart."*

Perhaps the most difficult time to express love for a child is when the fully alienated child is attacking you. Remember, it is part of the "show" to please the custodial parent. Don't blame the child. At that moment, say something like this:

"No matter what son, I love you deeply and always will."

Don't get caught up arguing with the child about whether you are a good parent or a bad parent. Try not to pay attention to the accusations. When time permits, you will address those issues. For now, let your child know that your love is still there and is unshakeable.

I would also suggest that you keep the following point in mind: if you are such a "bad person" already, what do you have to lose by expressing love to your child?

Nothing.

But that child has everything to gain by your reassurance.

Also keep in mind, that while telling the child that you love him or her is important, no message is more powerful than the behavior behind it. If the opportunity is there, don't just speak your love; show it.

The more you show your love to the child who is deprived of you, the more that child will come to know that the bond between you cannot be broken. It will only help your child get through the torture of not being with you.

DEMONSTRATING COMMITMENT

The pain of a visitation interference situation can often become so severe that the estranged parent feels tremendous urges to withdraw.

Do not.

The child who is being prevented from seeing you, needs you dearly. By withdrawing, you may signal to your child that you are not as loving and committed to the child as you would like your offspring to believe. In fact, the parent who may be trying to alienate you from your child will in essence succeed in what he or she is trying to do, if you withdraw.

Make a commitment to yourself that you will never abandon your child and that you will do everything you can to demonstrate your commitment to your child.

In the long run, it will pay off.

When you go to visit, if you are denied access time after time, keep going. Let your child see that you are trying. It's painful. But it shows your love.

If your ex-spouse is alienating your child from you, do not give fuel that can be added to the fire. Remember, if you do not come when you are scheduled to, your former partner could simply say to the child, "*I guess she just doesn't care about you anymore.*" Your absence only strengthens such a statement by a custodial parent.

Each time you go to see your child and your former spouse prevents it, your child is exposed to the episode. In time, your child will come to realize who is causing the problem. And when the time is right, that child will rebel against his or her jailkeeper.

For those of you who have a former spouse who puts your child in the middle, the urges to withdraw can be just as painful as the parent whose child is alienated. In either case, one must find the balance between demonstrating the commitment and taking care of yourself.

They are not mutually exclusive.

Don't abandon your child under the guise of "I have to take care of myself"; find a middle position. Find a "safer way" to communicate to your child. In the next few pages, you will see several examples of how to do this.

Remember: in your heart you may feel deeply committed to your child, but if you don't engage in the behaviors that demonstrate this to the child, then he or she cannot be confident of your commitment.

PRESENTING YOUR ANGUISH

A father who has been prevented from seeing his daughter for over a year tries to visit with her at school but the mother involved prevents him from seeing the child. Hurt, frustrated and angry, the father leaves the school premises, drives away and pulls to the side of the road to bawl his eyes out. That night, he writes a three page letter to his daughter and pours his heart out to her.

Stories such as this are told by nonresidential parents all over the country. The heartache experienced is intense. The emotions are diverse.

Sadness.

Anger.

Frustration.

Worry.

Guilt.

For present purposes, we can neatly summarize these and other relevant emotions as anguish.

In Chapter 23 we discussed how the parent denied visitation might go about handling the emotions that are aroused by visitation interference. In this section, I would like to address the issue of how one presents his or her anguish to the children involved.

First of all, I am not aware of any scientific evidence that addresses this problem. Thus, I can only offer my best advice.

Should a parent let a child know that the parent is suffering? This is not an easy question to answer. There are no clearly established rules which would allow us to say what is right and what is wrong.

Generally speaking, I believe it is best to spare children as much pain as one can. Childhood is a one-time opportunity. Adults have the experience and maturity to deal with pain. When a child can be spared the pain, he or she should be.

Unfortunately, some visitation interference situations cause such intense anguish in the denied parent that the pain cannot be concealed. On the other hand, there are times when children may need to know that their parent is in fact suffering with this ordeal. The parent who is severely pained but denies it to his or her child is in fact, lying. Thus, there is a basic dilemma here between sparing the child pain and being honest with the child about one's anguish.

There is no easy solution to this dilemma. On the one hand, keeping the child spared from unnecessary pain is a laudable goal. On the other hand, being dishonest in a relationship does not bode well.

I suggest a compromise position on this issue. When a child can be spared pain it seems appropriate to do so. However, this should not be at the expense of potentially damaging the relationship by not being truthful.

If the pain is so severe that it cripples the parent but the parent tries to deny it to the child, the child is likely to know the parent is being untruthful. This might damage the relationship. As such, the compromised position I am suggesting requires the parent to judge for oneself as to when or how to reveal one's discomfort about the visitation interference.

I like honesty.

I also like sparing children unnecessary pain.

Thus, if the parent feels the need to share his or her anguish, it should be done in a balanced way between honesty and not causing unnecessary pain.

When a parent expresses that he or she is in pain, the child will most likely experience pain as well. Fortunately, children do not experience emotional pain in the way that adults do and younger children do not have an attention span that would allow them to continue to experience anguish in as pervasive a manner as adults can experience it.

Generally speaking, I think it is best to reveal one's anguish in person.

The child should see your expressions.

The child should be able to experience your touch.

The child should be able to look into your eyes.

The child should be given the opportunity to cry along with you, if need be.

Unfortunately, in many visitation interference situations, the denied parent has no opportunity to share in person his or her psychological pain with the child. That only leaves a few other choices: the phone, a letter, or through another person. Each has significant drawbacks.

In an earlier section of this Chapter, I talked about demonstrating commitment. I emphasized how important it was to keep the doors open. If your limited interactions with your child are filled with you pouring out your emotions of pain, then over time these "visits" are likely to become dreaded by the child. In other words, if each interaction you have with the child is painful, in time, the child will not wish to have those interactions.

Thus, my advice is that if you need to reveal your pain through a letter, or on the phone, or through another person, then it should be limited in some way. Either you should seldom do it or, if you do it more than once, do not fill the entire communication with your anguish.

In certain cases, letting the child know that you think of them every day and cry from time to time, might be more palatable than letting the child know that you are seriously depressed and contemplating suicide.

As I said, there are no clear cut rules to follow when it comes to revealing the pain that you are experiencing due to the absence of your child.

Use your best judgment.

ATTACKING THE FORMER SPOUSE

As a general rule of thumb, it is usually best to avoid attacking the former spouse in front of the children. Children want to think well of their parents; attacks upon a parent hurts the child as well.

Unfortunately, it is not always easy.

During a heated custody battle over four children, a custodial parent repeatedly told the children that the nonresidential parent favored the oldest child over the three younger ones.

In this situation, the noncustodial parent *could* have taken the opportunity to respond with a statement like this:

> *"There she goes again, lying through the skin of her teeth to hurt me. I don't know why I put up with her crap all of these years! You know damn well this is a total lie! Sinners usually end up in Hell."*

A response like this, would certainly teach the children that a noncustodial parent had strong antagonistic feelings toward the custodial parent's claim. Unfortunately, such a response would strongly upset the children. A better response was demonstrated by the parent in question.

> *"Children, I love you all equally. I don't love any of you less than or more than the other. I have no favorite, because I have four favorites, each one of you."*

The father then invited the children to express their feelings and to give examples of any potential favoritism they thought might have been displayed. By handling the situation in this manner, the noncustodial parent was able to somewhat correct the accusation made without directly attacking the custodial parent (I say "somewhat" because the behavior of the custodial parent on this issue is not under the noncustodial parent's control).

Unfortunately, there are some situations that arise which leave no choice but to fight back against an unwarranted attack.

> A boy who had been kidnapped and later reunited with his father, was brainwashed to believe that his father had not given his mother any money for months. In a rage, the boy told his father that he hated him for " *... destroying our family.*" The father listened patiently, then reassuringly showed the child copies of all checks made out to his former spouse, documenting the substantial sums the mother had actually received from him.

In this particular example, the parent under attack calmly and gently provided objective evidence that the other parent's accusation was false. Most important, the attacked parent did not use the opportunity to barrage the child with complaints about the other parent.

Some situations require tougher responses.

A woman prevented the father of her children from seeing them for over six months. When the father finally got ahold of the children, they informed him that he was not their father, as their mother had told them.

In this situation, the father had no choice but to counter the serious lie that had been perpetrated to his children.

PROVIDING LEGAL INFORMATION

During a visitation and/or custody dispute, children want to know what is going on. This is especially true for children who are old enough to understand that the dispute between their parents is being played out in the judicial system. Children have a big stake in the legal proceedings. It is very tempting to share various pieces of legal information with them.

Unfortunately, the way legal information is provided to the children can be detrimental at times.

A parent who says to a child, *"My attorney says that she will not let your mother get away with that,"* is precisely the type of information a child should *not* hear. Parents who are intent on attacking the other parent often *selectively* use letters, Court Orders, or biased summaries of legal proceedings to his or her own advantage. When a child hears, *"My attorney says,"* the child assumes that it must be true; most children do not have the capability to understand that what an attorney may say may not be accurate either in its content or in its representation by someone else.

I think it is best to minimize discussions of what is going on legally but assure your child that you are *"working on it."* Say that you hope things will go the way you would like them to and that no matter what happens, you are sure that things will work out in the long run. As noted earlier, legal warfare can be incredibly stressful for parents; imagine what it can do to children if you embroil them into the specifics of it.

In certain cases, such as when one is dealing with a Divorce Related Malicious Parent Syndrome, it may be necessary to share a particular Court Order with a child. This should only be done under rare circumstances.

Note the following:

> A child had been brainwashed by her mother against her father. The Court removed the child from the mother and Ordered that there be no contact between the mother and child until after the mother received psychiatric evaluation and treatment. The father was having great difficulty helping the child to see that she had been brainwashed. After much unsuccessful effort, the father decided to let the child read the Court Order that documented the brainwashing efforts by the mother. Seeing this written and signed by a Judge in "black and white", enabled the child to begin questioning the lies that had been used by the mother against the father.

While the information and advice I have provided above may be useful, it should be noted that the Courtroom involvement of children in visitation and custody disputes appears to be undergoing change.

In Florida for example, there was recently a highly publicized case in which an adolescent female sued to seek a divorce from her biological parents. Clearly, in such a case the adolescent (with her own attorney), was privy to detailed information in her legal proceedings. Of course, this is a highly unusual case. Nevertheless, it suggests that the door has been opened to some unique involvement of children in visitation and custody disputes.

25

HANDLING OTHERS

In this Chapter I will discuss various strategies for dealing with others who become involved in a visitation interference and/or custody dispute.

YOUR ATTORNEY

You must have an excellent working relationship with a highly qualified attorney. If your attorney is not fully on your side, it is unlikely that he or she will achieve many of the goals that you have agreed upon.

Harassing your attorney will only come back at you.

Be as cooperative, helpful, and easy to get on with as you can be. If you act in this manner and pay your attorney the money that is due on a regular basis, he or she will certainly be on your side.

In a visitation interference situation, the more that you can document, the better. I suggest that you keep extensive notes and files on anything of relevance. I mean it: anything! You never know what will come in handy later on.

A young girl in a custody battle wrote a story about why she wanted to have the same occupation as one of her parents when she grows up. This item was later used to help dispel the other parent's claim that the daughter did not have much of an attachment to the parent being attacked.

In documenting things for your legal battle, it's always better to have more information to choose from than to have very little to choose from.

Organize this information so that when you meet with your attorney, you can present it as efficiently and clearly as possible. This will save you money and your attorney headaches.

Remember that no one is as close to the situation as you are.

Do not expect your attorney to remember all of the information you provide him or her.

Do not expect your attorney to keep up with all of the idiosyncrasies of your case.

In a complex visitation dispute, it is simply not possible.

Be your attorney's "top assistant" for your case!

If you have any concerns about whether or not you have selected the right attorney, I suggest that you reread Chapters 18 and 19.

OPPOSING COUNSEL

The attorney representing your former spouse has been hired to wage warfare, just as your attorney has been.

Your ex's attorney may call you a cheat.

Your ex's attorney may call you a liar.

You ex's attorney may falsely accuse you of all kinds of things.

Do not take it personally.

It is this attorney's job to attack you even if you are the nicest person in the world. I repeat: do not take it personally.

It is important for you to keep in mind that the attorney representing your former spouse may not be a bad person at all, even though you think this person is right down there with the Devil. It is this attorney's job to represent your former partner with his or her greatest skill.

I think the best approach towards dealing with the former spouse's attorney is to mentally prepare to handle him or her in the "correct" manner. By this, I mean the following:

> *It is to your advantage to treat your former spouse's attorney with the greatest understanding, cooperation, and forthrightness that your attorney will allow.*

Trying to anger the opposing counsel will only come back at you. If you act reasonable, courteous, and helpful in the Courtroom with the opposing counsel, it will only help you in the eyes of the Judge. It might also frustrate the opposing counsel.

I know that this sounds very hard to do.

That is because it is very hard to do.

Nevertheless, if you can achieve this mental attitude and execute the appropriate behavior in the Courtroom, it will be to your advantage.

In some cases, the opposing attorney will use all kinds of "tricks" to try to unsettle you. Your words may be twisted into something you never said or meant. Your answers may be greeted with laughter and mockery. Think of the most intimidating attorney you ever saw on television or in the movies and you can get an idea about what some of these "tricks" are.

Don't be coaxed in.

Remain calm, reasonable and cooperative—no matter how the former spouse's attorney behaves!

In Chapter 23, I talked about the importance of displaying *royal manners*.

Do so.

Especially in the Courtroom.

THE JUDGE

The Judge has all the power in the Courtroom.

Respect it at all times.

Never forget it. Not even for a moment.

In the Courtroom, always follow the directions of your attorney. He or she knows the proper procedure and etiquette. You are paying for expert advice and direction.

Use it.

During the proceedings remain seated and quiet.

Do not make faces, do not blurt out expletives, and do not bang the table. When your former spouse is lying, inform your attorney in a way that the two of you have agreed upon beforehand.

You will get your chance to speak later on.

When the Judge asks you a question, answer it immediately, with the most honest and useful response that you can give. If you feel like crying, do so; it will not hurt you. In fact, it very well might help the Judge feel more for you and your plight.

Do not threaten anyone.

Remain calm, reasonable and quiet. Respectful behavior is the only respectable behavior in the Courtroom.

THE GUARDIAN AD LITEM

When the Guardian Ad Litem (or Attorney Ad Litem) is conducting an evaluation to be reported to the Judge, you must treat him or her very much like you would treat the Judge.

The Guardian is in control.

Do not try to take over.

Be as honest and cooperative as you can. Try to present the best image possible but do not attempt to be someone you are not. Becoming adversarial with the Guardian does not get you very far. If you are legitimately being prevented from seeing your child, a good Guardian can be of tremendous help to you.

Unfortunately, if you get a "bad apple" (see Chapter 22) you may need to have your attorney engage in some "fancy footwork." This can range from your attorney telephoning the Guardian to offer some "friendly" advice, to a Motion to the Court to have the Guardian removed from the case.

THE MENTAL HEALTH PROFESSIONAL

Similar to the Guardian Ad Litem, the mental health professional that becomes involved in a visitation interference or custody dispute, wields a certain degree of power. Whether you like this person or not is irrelevant. You are trying to gain this person's cooperation to help you resolve the visitation interference.

Be cooperative, be honest, and most importantly, be yourself. If you try to fool the mental health professional, more than likely it will come back at you. If you have to take psychological tests, do so with honesty and accuracy. Certain psychological tests have scales on them to detect lying or deliberate attempts to present oneself in a phony way.

If your children will see the mental health professional, do not try to manipulate them to say anything or do anything they normally wouldn't. Observe the following:

Lawrence was an Administrator in a Mental Health Center. During an evaluation by a licensed psychologist for custody and visitation purposes, Lawrence coached his son on how to respond on a certain psychological test. When the son took the test, he followed his father's advice but inadvertantly "tipped off" the psychologist. When the psychologist asked the boy why he responded the way he did, the boy let it be known that he did it the way his father told him to. The father was not pleased with the final recommendations of the psychologist.

If you have any objective evidence or witnesses portraying the visitation interference behavior of your former spouse, alert the mental health professional to this information. However, first make sure if you should do this by discussing it beforehand with your attorney. The reason is this: Anything that you present to the mental health professional can potentially be brought up in Court. If your attorney prefers that you keep the information privileged between you and the attorney, follow his or her suggestion.

As I noted in Chapter 22, the mental health professional is restricted by the absence of strong scientific evidence regarding how to evaluate and treat visitation interference situations. Because of this, his or her biases will play a more important role than any scientific evidence will. Thus, it is important that you try to develop as good a relationship as you can with the mental health professional who has become involved in your case.

THE TEACHER

Whenever possible, stay in contact with the teachers of your children. When you can go to parent teacher conferences, do so. If you can call him or her on the phone, do so. Ask that copies of grades and any other reports of significance be forwarded to you.

Be as nice and cooperative as you can with your children's teachers. Remember: they spend alot of time with your children. They are often overworked and under paid. Their jobs can be stressful. Try not to add to their stress. If a teacher is not being cooperative with you, do not threaten the individual. Try to cooperatively work it out. Only if you cannot work it out in an amicable way with the teacher, should you approach a school administrator.

THE SCHOOL PRINCIPAL

The school buildings and school personnel are like a little kingdom of the school Principal. Keep this in mind. He or she requires the appropriate level of respect.

It is best to try to avoid situations that require you to interact with the school Principal. However, in visitation interference disputes, the school Principal will often become involved.

As I mentioned in Chapter 23, try to utilize *royal manners.* Be reasonable, helpful, respectful, and honorable.

Do not attack.

Do not threaten.

Do not burn down a school building.

Should you be unable to achieve the goal that you have aimed for with the school Principal, the next step is to approach the school board of the county in which the school is located.

Ask to speak to the person in charge of "Student Information" or "Student Evaluation." Each school board has its own hierarchy of who is in charge of whom and each has it own system of giving titles to these people. If need be, ask for "The person in charge of the Principals at the local schools." You might even need to meet with the school board's attorney. Hopefully, you will not need to push the issue all the way up to the head of the county school board.

Unfortunately, not all school Principals are cooperative and helpful. Let me give an example.

A nonresidential father was being prevented from seeing his children by his former spouse. The father tried to maintain contact with the children by visiting them at school. The interfering parent relocated so that the schools the children attended were not in the same county as the father. When the father went to visit at each school, the mother continued to try to interfere. Neither Principal wanted to get in the middle. The Principal at the youngest child's school, was very helpful and cooperative to the father. The Principal at the other school made it clear that he did not want to be bothered with the situation; he informed the father of the presence of police on the school grounds and that there would be no hesitancy in having the father arrested, if so desired.

When you approach the school administrator, do so with *royal manners.*

RELATIVES

Your relatives are your children's relatives. Your former spouse's relatives are your children's relatives. Try not to publicly attack your spouse's relatives; it is an indirect attack on your spouse which in a way, is an attack on your children.

Sometimes, this advice is hard to follow.

A child in a custody battle was told by his maternal grandfather that the boy's father, *"deserved to have his legs broken."*

In another example:

A contestant in a custody battle falsely told the children that the other parent's father, *"had hallucinations"* and was *"mentally disturbed."*

These are precisely the kind of behaviors that should be avoided when one becomes involved in a custody or visitation dispute. The children need to be spared from such unnecessary pain.

Where possible, one should try to keep relationships open and cordial, even with your former spouse's relatives. When it is possible, everyone benefits.

However, sometimes it is not possible.

A father in a custody dispute was extremely close with the uncle of his former spouse; their relationship spanned over a decade. They kissed when they greeted each other, in the traditional European way. One day the uncle told the father that he could no longer speak with him because his niece had threatened to have nothing to do with the uncle if he was to speak with the divorcing father. Needing to keep peace in his own family, the uncle regrettably removed his relationship from the father in the custody battle.

In this example, not only did two people lose a good relationship unnecessarily, when visitation interference developed, the uncle was not able to participate in mediating the problem.

FRIENDS

Like relatives, the same rules apply to friends. Unfortunately, when a visitation interference dispute has developed, many friends will take one side of the dispute or withdraw from the dispute in its entirety.

Two families were close until one couple became involved in a custody battle. One member of the divorcing couple, began to engage in visitation interference. The other couple took the side of the interfering parent because that parent was still responsible for car pools of all the children involved. The parent denied visitation was denied the friendship of the other family as well.

Sometimes it is easy to predict which friends will remain connected and which friends won't.
Other times, it is impossible.
In either case, when friends leave a situation that involves visitation interference, it unfortunately reduces the number of people who might be of some potential help in handling the problem.

PARENTS OF OTHER CHILDREN

I recommend that one deal with parents of other children in the same way that one would deal with teachers, Principals, attorneys, Guardians and Judges: show them *royal manners.*
Remember that some will be cooperative and others will not be.
Some parents of other children would like to get involved to satisfy their own motivations; others will avoid involvement.
It is not always easy to predict.

A mother of a child on a tennis team who had no interactions with the father of another child on the tennis team, immersed herself in the custody battle of the other child. This woman testified in Court that she observed the father cursing the mother in question, when in fact, the incident never occurred.

This example helps to illustrate the extent to which others may be willing to violate societal norms in order to satisfy one's own motivational needs.

The mother who lied in Court had no relationship or interactions with the father in question, yet she was willing to violate the law by perjuring herself. Obviously, she had some need of her own to deal with.

As noted above, it is not always easy to predict who will and who won't get involved in such ways.

DOCTORS

Some parents who are illegitimately denied access to their children, often have to resort to medical records to gain information about the health of their offspring.

Unfortunately, doctors, dentists and the like have no desire to immerse themselves in a visitation interference dispute. Accordingly, such individuals should be treated carefully and diplomatically. However, if you provide the appropriate documentation, they will in fact provide the information that legally they must. No doctor wishes to be involved in a law suit.

By the same token, time is money and the more time spent on your situation, the less money goes in the doctor's pocket.

Some doctors will have staff that will tell you when your child's next appointment is scheduled for. If you can find this out in advance, you can wait outside to try and see your child. You can even go in the waiting room.

Do not create a scene!

Be aware that the doctor and his or her staff may not be as cooperative as you would like. In fact, there are times when you may not even know that they are not being cooperative until it is too late.

A noncustodial parent who was denied visitation by the custodial parent, called the dentist's office to find out when the children would be coming for their next appointment. The receptionist did not know but promised to call the noncustodial parent as soon as an appointment was made. She never called. The children's appointment came and went. When the noncustodial parent called back to check, it was six months until the next scheduled appointment.

Attacking or threatening the doctor's staff would not lead to much cooperation. A polite reminder and/or request seems most appropriate.

As the reader can see, dealing with a serious visitation interference problem can be like running an obstacle course. Many hurdles have to be leaped. If you handle others in the way that I am suggesting, the hurdles may not be so difficult to overcome.

26

HANDLING METHODS OF VISITATION INTERFERENCE

In Chapter 2, I outlined a variety of methods that are engaged in by a custodial parent aimed at interfering with the visitation of the noncustodial parent. In this Chapter, I will discuss how to handle some of these methods. At this point, some readers may find it helpful to review Chapter 2 before proceeding.

As I discuss the visitation interference techniques in the present Chapter, the strategies that I suggest will probably be of some help to you. Unfortunately, I am unable to guarantee it. In extreme visitation interference situations, you may need the advice of multiple professionals.

HOME VISITATION INTERFERENCE

In the "unannounced — not at home" method, the nonresidential parent spends the time, energy, and emotions to carry through with visitation. When he or she arrives, the children are not there; the residential parent deliberately failed to inform the visiting parent that this would be the case.

One way to deal with this is to bring a book or a musical tape or CD along, and sit in one's car until the children come home. When they do, merely mention that you were there to see them but that there had been a misunderstanding about when that would be. This way, the children see that you are trying and that you care for them.

Another approach is to have your attorney seek a date specific, time specific, and location specific, visitation schedule. Draw it up in detail and have your attorney try to convince the Judge that this is the best arrangement to prevent a visitation interference situation.

If the former spouse continues to violate the date specific, time specific, and location specific visitation schedule, then it would be appropriate to ask your attorney to seek a supervised transfer point for visitation. In other words, your attorney would seek a Court Order that all transfers of the children are to be done on the agreed upon schedule in front of a neutral witness.

In the "not here —don't come" approach, the custodial parent merely informs the nonresidential parent that the children will not be there at the specified time. The options for dealing with this situation are similar to what was described with the "unannounced — not at home" method.

Dealing with the "smoke screen" technique can be difficult. Recall that here, when the noncustodial parent arrives to pick up the children, the residential parent engages the former spouse in an argument and then retreats into the house.

The best way to deal with this technique is to not argue. In fact, the nonresidential parent should merely ignore the behavior of the custodial parent. Say nothing, other than something like this: *"Please send the children out, I will wait by my car."*

If the former spouse continues ranting and raving, try to ignore this behavior but every once in a while, in a calm voice, say, *"please send out the children."*

When this is going on, more than likely the children are peering through the window or have their ears glued to the door. They will know that you are there wanting to visit with them.

This is important.

The best way to handle the "smoke screen" game, is to not get "sucked into playing" it.

In the, "changed locations" method, the custodial parent leaves a note informing the nonresidential parent that the locations for visitation transfer have changed and then it becomes impossible for the noncustodial parent to track down precisely where the children are.

Be sure to keep the note; it may prove useful in Court.

The best approach to handle the "changed locations" technique is to obtain a date specific, time specific, and location specific, visitation Court Order. If need be, the transfer should be done under supervision.

The same is true for the "schedule lie" maneuver. The reader may recall that in this ploy, the residential parent claims that there is a mistake as to when he or she is supposed to give up the children.

The "upset child" routine, where the custodial parent states that the child is "too upset to see you" can best be handled by a supervised transfer situation.

The same is true for several of the other home visitation interference situations; that is, the use of Court Orders for highly specified visitation schedules with a neutral transfer site and supervisor.

This can be helpful with the "other activity" method, the "running late" maneuver, the "multiple schedule" tactic, and the "incompatible schedule" technique.

TELEPHONE VISITATION INTERFERENCE

When a custodial parent utilizes the "hurry up" technique, the child is quickly guided off the telephone just a few minutes into the conversation with the nonresidential parent. The options for dealing with this method are limited.

One option is for the nonresidential parent to continue to call back. This may need to be done repeatedly.

A second option is for the noncustodial parent to instruct the child to call back. This approach assumes that since there is some communication, it should continue.

In the "excuse" maneuver, each time the noncustodial parent calls to speak with the child, he or she is told that the child is busy and unable to come to the phone. This is also a difficult ploy to get around. Nevertheless, there are two approaches worthy of consideration.

First, if you are aware of the schedule of the custodial parent, you may discover that there is a certain day and/or time when the child is in the house without the custodial parent. If such a situation exists, this would be an excellent time to place your phone calls.

The other approach worth considering is to have someone other than yourself call the child. Perhaps the custodial parent would allow the child to talk with one of your parents, relatives, or friends. Once the child is on the phone, the person who made the call can simply hand the phone to you.

These two approaches can also be used with the "hang up," "no message," and "hold on" techniques (see Chapter 4).

When the custodial parent utilizes the "stand by" technique, he or she provides strong hints to the child that the child should get off the phone with the nonresidential parent. As these clues are non-verbal, such as tapping a foot or looking angry, the nonresidential parent has no direct way to know what is going on. Since the child learns to get off the phone without being "told" to do so by the custodial parent, there is very little that the nonresidential parent can do. However, if the nonresidential parent is aware that the other parent is using the "stand by" method, then he or she might say something like this to the child:

> *"I know that you are under pressure not to talk with me right now...I understand and I love you very much."*

Finally, the reader may recall the "aversive conversation" technique. Here, the custodial parent screams, yells, and/or curses at, or tries to argue with, the nonresidential parent when calling to speak to the child. A good way to handle this method is to try to ignore the behavior of the custodial parent, wait out the storm, and every once in a while calmly repeat, *"May I speak to my daughter, please"* or, *"Please put Steven on the phone now."*

Another way to respond is to hang up. Then, wait awhile, and call back later. You may get lucky—the other parent may calm down or may have gone out.

MAIL VISITATION INTERFERENCE

The parent intent on interfering with mail visitation can do so easily, as he or she generally controls incoming and outgoing mail. However, let me share some methods worth trying to combat mail interference.

To get mail to your child, some approaches to consider are as follows:

First, address the envelope in a different handwriting. Since the custodial parent is familiar with your handwriting, you may want to ask someone else to address it or perhaps to type it.

Second, either put a return address on the envelope that the custodial parent is not familiar with, or do not provide a return address.

Third, consider sending your letters using certified return receipt mail.

If the child actually signs for the letter, then you know it was received.

Fourth, have your letter hand delivered. Do it yourself or have someone who has access to the child deliver it for you. Deliver it only to the child and not to the custodial parent. In some cases, you might be able to do this at the child's dance lesson, T-ball game or school.

In regard to the mail interference techniques employed by a custodial parent to prevent the child from sending mail to you, you can try to arm the child with several envelopes that are addressed to you and already stamped.

For those of you whose children are computer active, you might try to exchange E-mail.

Unfortunately, the parent who is fully committed to interfering with your mail visitation, can find ways around each of the techniques I have described in this section. However, if you are not dealing with a severe case such as those presented by parents with Parental Alienation Syndrome or Divorce Related Malicious Parent Syndrome, then some of these methods outlined may prove useful to you.

SCHOOL VISITATION INTERFERENCE

Custodial parents committed to blocking out the nonresidential parent from school related information may engage in the "false information," "black out," or "sole contact" maneuvers. In each of these cases, the custodial parent controls the flow of information about the child's schooling, special school programs, and other school related activities. The best way to handle this approach is to eliminate the custodial parent as the "middle man."

I would advise you to open up direct communication with each of the teachers in your child's school. Additionally, get to know the school secretary and instruct that person to provide you with the information. If needed, meet with the school Principal to make the necessary arrangements. Most importantly, follow the guidelines I outlined in Chapter 25 on dealing with teachers and school personnel.

When the custodial parent utilizes the "legal threat" ploy, you are most likely going to need an attorney to handle this for you. Most important, do not display any anger towards the school or its personnel. They are merely doing what they believe is their duty: follow the law and protect the child . They do not expect that a parent would lie about legal documents, although school personnel highly experienced with Parental Alienation Syndrome parents or Divorced Related Malicious Parent Syndrome cases may recognize the possibility of such fabrications.

In dealing with this particular problem, display *royal manners*. Be persistent but pleasant. By displaying this type of behavior along with the advice and direction of your attorney, the issue should be able to be cleared up in a short period of time; sooner or later, the truth will emerge regarding your former partner's claim about these so called legal documents.

When a custodial parent utilizes the "promoting discomfort" technique to interfere with school visitation, things can get very emotional and complicated. When the custodial parent tries to make people so uncomfortable with your presence on the campus, there are really only two things you can do.

First, do not "play." If the custodial parent is trying to engage you in an argument, simply do not engage in it.

Ignore it.

If on the other hand, the teachers and/or Principals have been harassed to keep you off the campus, then be sure to follow the advice given for handling the "legal threat" ploy:

Act calm, reasonable, and cooperative.
Have your attorney get involved.

When a custodial parent uses the "valued volunteer" strategy to gain enough power within the school setting to prevent your visitation, you have few options available to combat it.

First, try to negotiate with the school Principal. You might take an approach like this:

> *"Thank you for meeting with me. I wish to cause no difficulty for you or your staff, I merely hope to be able to see my child. I understand that my ex-wife is an important volunteer here at your school. I think that is great. However, she seems to be using her position here to prevent me from seeing my child. I would like to work this out in the most easy, reasonable, and fair way possible. What I propose is this: Let*

us take one day per week that I can come to have lunch with my daughter and the other four days my ex-wife can spend with my daughter. When it is my ex-wife's days, I promise not to appear on the school grounds. On the day that I am to visit with my daughter, please have my ex-wife not be anywhere near the classroom or lunchroom during those times. This should avoid any possible conflicts on the school grounds. I think that this is a fair and easy to follow proposition and I would very much appreciate it if you could help us to achieve this. It certainly is in my child's best interest."

Should the school Principal be uncooperative, I would suggest you contact an appropriate person at the school board. If this does not work, then you might try having your attorney mediate some type of solution.

In some situations, your contact may be reduced to having someone at the school pass on messages from you to your child. Letters, brief notes, or any other items that you can get through, should be sent.

If all else fails, I recommend that you continue to go to the school even if you only get to wave at your child. While 5 seconds of interaction may not seem like much, when a child is being denied access to a parent, those 5 seconds are treasured.

In this way, the child knows that you have not given up and that the child is cared about.

OUTSIDE ACTIVITIES VISITATION INTERFERENCE

When you are trying to visit with your child in outside activities such as organized sports, meetings, lessons, or ceremonies, the more you know about the events, the better you can plan for action.

Clearly, do not rely on your former spouse for accurate information. Get it from the "horse's mouth."

Call the gymnastics academy and find out when the child's show will be.

Meet the swimming coach and obtain a copy of the team schedule.

Know what time the school play starts and ends.

And so on.

Where possible, arrive at the event early enough so that your child can potentially interface with you on the way into the event. Follow a similar strategy on the way out of the event.

If the custodial parent engages in the "barrier" technique, do not try to "break through" the shield being provided by the custodial parent and/or the other accomplices. Your goal is to let your child know that you are there and that you love your child. Wave to your little one.

Blow a kiss your child's way.

Smile lovingly when your child gazes in your direction.

The last thing that you want to do is to engage in a major conflict with your former spouse in front of your child. If your child sees that you are trying, and that you are not the cause of the problem, it will go a long way in your relationship down the road.

Finally, when the custodial parent has successfully taught the "child knows" method, you should be prepared for rejection directly by the child.

He or she may say to you, *"I don't want to see you."*

Your gaze might be avoided.

Your child may even ignore you.

Try not take it personally. Understand that the child must do this in order to satisfy the custodial parent and to escape that parent's wrath.

Whenever possible, say to the child something like this:

> *"I love you darling. I will never stop trying to see you. You look fantastic! Take good care and I will keep trying to see you. I love you. Bye."*

Such an interaction may take 10 seconds but its comfort to the child may last for quite a while. More importantly, the value of your continued interest will last a lifetime.

=27====

MANAGING SEVERE
METHODS OF VISITATION
INTERFERENCE

In this Chapter I will discuss strategies for managing three extreme aspects of visitation interference:

1) Combating a Parental Alienation Syndrome or a Divorced Related Malicious Parent Syndrome;
2) Handling abuse allegations; and
3) Dealing with kidnapping.

PARENTAL ALIENATION SYNDROME AND DIVORCE RELATED MALICIOUS PARENT SYNDROME

Dealing with a hostile and manipulative person can be quite stressful. When such an individual controls the daily lives of your children, the stress gets even worse.

In this type of situation, the methods that I have outlined in Section Eight should be utilized. These methods form the basis for how to deal with extreme cases. However, I would like to emphasize six particular points.

First, you must try working with a good attorney on this issue. If you are lucky, your hard work will get you some degree of satisfaction through the judicial system. Unfortunately, in certain cases, the legal system cannot handle the problem. However, you will never know if your case could be successfully managed by the judicial system, unless you try.

Second, do not withdraw from your child. Continue to show your child that you keep trying to see him or her.

Go to the schools.

Go to the team games.

Go to the doctor's office.

Do what you need to do, even if your interactions are limited to just a few seconds at each exposure.

Third, when necessary, keep your visits with your child in public. There are two reasons for this.

(1) if your former spouse creates a scene and there is a witness, that might be useful to you in the Courtroom.

(2) even if your former spouse is not present, that does not prevent him or her from making a false allegation of abuse from your visits with the child. By doing so in public, you are improving your chances of surviving a false abuse accusation.

Fourth, keep your relationship with your child alive *in your life.* By this I mean, keep your child's presence in your daily experiences.

Put report cards on the refrigerator.

Carry pictures in your wallet.

Find a nice photo of you and your child and have it blown up for a poster in your home.

Keep his or her belongings in the place where they were last left.

Continue to collect things for your child. Store them away for him or her.

Do not torture yourself — but do not abandon your child either.

Fifth, avoid the former spouse whenever possible. In extreme cases, sometimes the visitation interfering spouse is doing so because he or she wants to still have a relationship with you, even if it may be a "sick" one. The more you allow the adversarial parent to abuse you through your children, the more it encourages that parent. Thus, wherever possible, avoid that individual.

Finally, take care of yourself. You need to stay as healthy as you can to improve your success at surviving this ordeal. If your exposures to your child are few and marred by you looking ill, this will only upset the child.

The more you take care of yourself, the better it will be for both you and your child down the road.

Remember, you have a future together.
Never forget it!

ABUSE ALLEGATIONS

As noted in Chapter 11, if you are falsely accused of abusing your own child, you may become highly victimized by the system. If the abuse allegation is taken seriously, you are unfortunately in for one of the most stressful periods of your life.

Rule number one: Play the game. You have no choice in the matter. If you are falsely accused, your child has been taken away, and legal proceedings against you are unfolding, running away will not solve anything. You must play the game.

Rule number two: The attorney representing you in this issue is absolutely critical. Reread Chapters 18, and 19, which cover attorney and judicial issues.

Rule number three: Learn as much as you can about the process. Know what is in store for you. Research it as best as you can. Talk with appropriate officials of the state agency that is involved. Identify appropriate mental health personnel with experience in the area. Contact organizations that assist victims of false accusations (for example, The False Memory Syndrome Foundation in Philadelphia). Read whatever you can get your hands on that is relevant. And most important, follow the directions of your attorney.

In some cases, you may need to hire an expert on visitation interference and abuse allegations to assist your attorney in developing both offensive and defensive strategies.

Finally, there is no greater time than this one to diligently display *royal manners* (See Chapter 23).

KIDNAPPING

Parental kidnapping of a child is a serious matter. It is against the law. Unfortunately, it's more common than one would think. As we saw in Chapter 12, over 300,000 family related kidnappings were reported in 1991.

When a family member kidnaps a child, it can be devastating. To increase the chances of finding your child, you must engage in a variety of important steps.

First, contact the appropriate law enforcement personnel in your area. These include the following:

The local police department.
The county police department.
The state police department.
The Federal Bureau of Investigation (FBI).

Second, you should contact the Attorney General's office in the state that you reside in.

Third, contact the National Center For Missing And Exploited Children. This is a private, not-for-profit agency that was established by the United States Congress. The National Center for Missing and Exploited Children works in conjunction with the United States Department of Justice; it is located in Arlington, Virginia.

Fourth, contact Child Find Of America. This not-for-profit corporation is a charity whose mission is to help locate missing children. Child Find Of America has helped to find missing children in the United States and in other countries. There are no charges for their services. Child Find Of America is located in New Paltz, New York.

These organizations can take you step by step through the process of trying to identify the whereabouts of your child and to help return your child to you.

Finally, you may wish to hire a private investigator. I suggest you find one who has a proven track record in similar cases.

SECTION NINE

CONCLUDING COMMENTS

In this final section of the book, I will adress a variety of important issues raised by the problem of child visitation interference.

In Chapter 28, I outline a number of important areas for the scientific community to address.

In Chapter 29, I discuss several key issues facing society as we begin to deal with the difficulties generated by child visitation interference.

=28

SCIENTIFIC ISSUES

Throughout this book, I have emphasized the lack of scientific research on visitation interference. In this Chapter, I will address some of the important tissues that need to be addressed through the process of science.

THE IMPORTANCE OF RESEARCH

Why is science so important for dealing with child visitation interference? The answer is simple: without scientific findings, we are left to act from the opinions of others.

Why should that be such a problem?

Because opinions can be wrong.

A long time ago, if someone believed you were a witch, certain people in authority held the following opinion:

> *"If we throw you into a lake and you drown, then you are not a witch. If you do not drown, then you must be a witch and therefore, must be executed."*

See why opinions by those in authority can sometimes be dangerous?

Research attempts to establish facts. With well established facts, we are more able to handle problems than without those facts. Imagine if we had tried to go to the moon without any research. We never would have gotten there.

To resolve the crisis of child visitation interference, we need to develop hard facts about the problem.

The bottom line is this:

The more high quality research that can be supported on child visitation interference, the more likely we are to resolve the difficulties imposed upon us.

AREAS FOR RESEARCH

What kind of research should be conducted on child visitation interference?

I will try to answer this in the remaining sections of this Chapter. However, it is important to understand that not all scientists would necessarily agree with all of the recommendations I will make.

Scientists often disagree with each other. This is particularly true when there are few facts available on a particular topic. When there are few facts available, scientists must resort to their own opinions; we have already discussed how opinions can potentially pose serious problems for us.

Despite the above, I believe that most scientists who would consider the suggestions that I am making, would agree that these are reasonable and useful topics for research investigations.

MEASUREMENT

One cannot conduct research on a particular topic unless one can measure the event one is studying. The better the measurement, the more likely the research will be of higher quality.

Let us take the problem of measuring visitation interference.

In the first Section of this book, I reviewed a study by Dr. Joyce Arditti, showing that 50 percent of fathers report their former spouse interfering with visitation. I also told you about research that was reviewed by Dr. Kenneth Kressel, revealing that 40 percent of mothers admitted denying visitation in order to punish their former spouse. In both of these studies, we have depended on reports of mothers and fathers who are involved in a heated conflict.

Are the reports of these mothers and fathers accurate?

Not necessarily.

In a 1991 study by Braver and associates that was published in the *American Journal of Orthopsychiatry*, it was found that mothers were likely to *under-report* how often they interfere with visitation. It was also found that fathers were more likely to *exaggerate* how often their former spouses interfered with visitation.

Does that mean that the 40 percent figure reported by mothers and the 50 percent figure reported by fathers is inaccurate?

Does it mean that the frequency of visitation interference is 45 percent?

Is it lower?

Is it higher?

These questions can be better answered if we develop a more objective measure of visitation interference.

When we do research and ask people to report on something they have experienced, their reports are not always accurate.

Sometimes people can't remember.

Sometimes people remember something incorrectly.

Sometimes people deliberately lie.

The point is, that when we base our findings only on the self-report of others, there is likely to be some error involved. This is especially true when the subjects in the research have a vested interest in the problem (like parents who are involved in a visitation interference situation).

To really get a precise figure of visitation interference, we need to use more objective measures. Let me illustrate this with an example.

In Section Eight of this book, I discussed the use of having certain visitation transfers conducted under supervision. In other words, when one parent transfers the children to the other parent for visitation, a neutral third party is present to supervise it. Such a neutral person might be able to give us a more accurate measurement of visitation interference than the self-reports of the mothers and fathers involved.

Imagine further that in the supervised transfer situation, each parent was required to "sign in" at each transfer of the children. If we waited a few months, and then asked each parent separately, *"How often did your spouse interfere with visitation?"* we could find out certain things.

First, we could compare the self-reports of the mothers and fathers to each other, and also to the data reported by the neutral supervisor of transfers.

We could also compare each of these to the number of actual signatures for each parent.

In this way, we are more likely to get a better measurement of the frequency of visitation interference.

While there are many ways to go about measuring this type of behavior, I think the above example gives the reader a general idea about the kinds of research that needs to be done.

CLASSIFICATION

When you have an irritation on the skin of your arm, there may be several different reasons why the irritation has appeared.

It might be due to a fungal infection.

Perhaps it is due to an allergy.

It might be a side effect of a medication you are taking.

The point is, that when you have a particular problem, such as a skin irritation, it is important to know what type of problem, what type of skin irritation you have. If it is a fungal infection, it will be treated differently than if it is due to an allergy.

This little example helps to illustrate the importance of having a good classification system.

If we know the different types that are in the classification system, then we are more likely to learn what things occur with type A and what things occur with type B. We are then more likely to know what things we can do about problems with type A and what things we can do about problems with type B.

In medicine, we refer to this as diagnosis. Diagnosis is merely a classification system. In order for any field of science to progress, one must have a good classification system.

In the area of child visitation interference, I believe it is important that we develop a good classification system.

You will note that I have used my own classification system throughout this book. For example, I gave names to some of the techniques of visitation interference. I also categorized some of the areas where visitation interference occurs, such as at home and at school.

These are merely my opinions.

Of course, they are based on my observations and experiences.

Research will eventually tell us whether my classification system is useful or not. At the moment, I would guess that it is useful. I am not aware that any other classification system on this topic currently exists. However, I would hope that after 20 years of research, my opinions of today on this topic would be seen as obsolete. This would please me, because it would mean that we have developed important facts through science.

It very well may turn out that the person who is a telephone visitation interfering parent is different than a parent who engages in school visitation interference. Similarly, we may find that what causes a Parental Alienation Syndrome is quite different from what causes a Divorce Related Malicious Parent Syndrome to develop.

By having a good classification system for child visitation interference, we are more likely to establish better facts about this important problem.

THE EFFECTS OF INTERFERENCE

At the present time, we do not have any solid research findings on the long-term effects of visitation interference on the children involved. However, most professionals would agree that the effects are unlikely to be positive.

Speculating on this issue, it would seem probable that children who come from the homes of Divorced Related Malicious Parent Syndrome, are more likely to have psychological problems as adults compared to children who are not raised in such homes.

On the other side of the coin, it is also possible that mild visitation interference may have no long term negative effects on the children.

The answers are presently unknown.

The research needs to be done.

By being able to measure child visitation interference well and by being able to classify different types of visitation interference correctly, we are more likely to be able to try to answer important questions like what the effects of visitation interference are on children.

PREVENTION

The ultimate goal of any health related field is to prevent whatever problems the field is geared toward resolving.

The psychiatrist ultimately aims to prevent schizophrenia.

The oncologist ultimately aims to prevent cancer.

The dentist aims to prevent tooth decay.

Our goal is to prevent child visitation interference from ever taking place.

How do we go about doing this?

First, we need to be able to accurately measure child visitation interference. Then we need to be able to know what types of visitation interference patterns there are. After we accomplish this, we need to investigate what the causes of child visitation interference are. This hopefully would lead us to a position where we could begin to test programs that try to prevent visitation interference from occurring in the first place.

In the long run, prevention is usually a cheaper alternative than trying to treat problems that already exist. A good example can be found in the public health literature.

There was once a time when small pox would kill many, many individuals. Today, an effective vaccine is available that prevents the disease from occurring.

How many people do you know that have small pox?

If we truly aim to prevent child visitation interference, our best bet is to encourage as much research as possible.

29

SOCIETAL ISSUES

Child visitation interference is a societal issue. As we noted very early in this book, the problem may touch the lives of one out of every five Americans. Child visitation interference shows itself in our schools, in our homes, in our playgrounds, and in our Courtrooms.

In this Chapter, I will discuss a variety of issues that are raised for our society by the plague of child visitation interference.

PUBLIC AWARENESS

The title of this particular section is, "Public Awareness." Perhaps it would be better retitled as, "The Lack Of Public Awareness."

I am not sure why there has been little attention paid to child visitation interference in our society. I can't recall ever reading an article exclusively focused on it in the newspaper. I think I might have seen some minor references to child visitation problems in a handful of articles on divorced families. Once in a TV documentary on false allegations of sexual abuse it was mentioned. Just the other day, a dear cousin of mine told me she had seen a discussion of the problem on one of the daily TV talk shows.

It seems that the popular media is just beginning to talk about child visitation interference.

It is interesting that when I speak with a parent who is being denied access to his or her child, often the parent seems to have no idea that many other parents are suffering with the same problem. In fact, when I mention that it appears that millions of parents are affected by this problem, the parent in question appears very surprised.

The same thing seems to hold true when I speak to a relative of a parent who has been chronically denied visitation with a child. Sometimes when I inform the relative of the commonality of this problem, I get a look of surprise and a statement like, "Really? ... it's not just her?"

Many colleagues in the mental health professions also seem to be unaware of the nature and extent of the problem. Again, I do not know why that is.

Perhaps it is due to the lack of research available today on child visitation interference. It may also be due to the fact that there are very few descriptions in the professional literature of the problem and its nature. Of course, the writings of Dr. Gardner which were reviewed earlier, are an exception.

Perhaps the lack of attention to child visitation interference in the scientific and professional literature is part of the reason that the popular media has yet to provide ample accounts to the public.

Hopefully, this book will help to change that.

GENDER BIAS

Many women complain that the Courts are stacked against them. Some point out that there are fewer female Judges than male ones. Others point out that there is sometimes sexist language used and at other times actual sexual harassment towards them.

Men also complain that the Court system is stacked against them. Many fathers will tell you that they feel that Judges do not believe that fathers make good custodial parents. Other men will tell you that if you really want to understand discrimination based on gender, just experience being falsely accused of sexual abuse.

Interestingly, both men and women often complain that Court Ordered child support discriminates against them.

Following divorce, women frequently find that their standard of living goes down; men often find that they cannot afford the amount of child support the Court has mandated to be paid.

The bottom line is that *few people disagree about the presence of gender discrimination in the legal system. They just seem to disagree about who is actually being discriminated against.*

What about child visitation?

In 1992, the *Georgia State University Law Review* published a very interesting article on gender bias in the legal system. It was based on the work of a commission that was set up specifically to study this particular problem. After investigating, the commission created a report to the Supreme Court of Georgia. The report was then published.

Let me discuss some of their findings.

First, it appears that some fathers are discriminated against when they are noncustodial parents in regard to their visitation allotment. A father who has been involved in the day to day upbringing of his children for years may all of a sudden be allowed to see his children only every other weekend.

A *second* finding is that men's violence towards women and children, sometimes is not carefully considered when decisions about visitation are made. Some custodial mothers report that abusive fathers need to be carefully monitored beyond what the custodial mother is able to do on her own.

A *third* finding was that the Court seems to enforce child support more strongly than it does visitation rights.

A *fourth* conclusion was that the parent who interferes with visitation often may bring on non-payment of child support by the parent being denied access to the child.

Finally, relocating a child by the custodial parent without the noncustodial parent's permission was also viewed as another area of potential discrimination.

SYSTEM REFORM

Many complain about the way that child visitation interference is handled in the judicial system. Many also complain about the way child visitation interference is handled in the schools. It would seem that significant change needs to occur.

But what?

Take the issue of the custodial parent who has prevented the nonresidential parent from visiting with the child. Should the Judge put the primary residential parent in jail?

On the one hand, it would certainly punish the parent for interfering with visitation.

On the other hand, putting the custodial parent in jail could harm the child. It might also harm the noncustodial parent, who may not be in a financial position to take over as full custodian and to maintain a full time job as well.

The issue is clearly a complex one.

There is little doubt that the absence of strong punishment for child visitation interference creates a terrible dilemma. A noncustodial parent who is prevented continuously from seeing his or her child, may have to spend a small fortune to try to achieve results in the legal system. Unfortunately, spending the money may not necessarily achieve what one hopes to obtain.

Does it seem right that one should have to pay exorbitantly (or at all, for that matter) in order to see one's child when one already has the right to do so?

Of course not.

I suspect that in the future, Court Orders for child visitation will become very date, time, and location specific. The police may come to play a greater role in enforcing child visitation than they do at present. Clearly, they will need to be trained in how to handle these situations.

I also suspect that supervision centers will have to be created to develop an efficient system and location for ensuring transfers of children. School teachers and administrators will need to be trained in how to deal with the problem of visitation interference. So will mental health professionals. And Judges.

A new generation of experts will have to be developed.

There is little doubt that setting these changes in place will require a substantial investment of education and research dollars.

ECONOMIC CONCERNS

Child visitation interference appears to be a costly problem. Families spend thousands of dollars on attorney fees. Mental health professionals may soak up significant amounts of money as well. Guidance counselors in schools need to be paid. The list goes on and on.

I am not an economist and therefore am unable to adequately estimate what the financial burden of child visitation interference is.

How does one calculate pain and suffering of this type?

How does one adequately measure lost productivity at work due to depression in a parent denied access to his or her child?

These issues will eventually be considered by experts in our society as the public becomes more attuned to the problem of child visitation interference.

RESEARCH AND PREVENTION

Throughout this book, I have emphasized the importance of scientific research in tackling the child visitation interference problem. In Chapter 28, I pointed out that prevention programs are the ultimate goal of such an effort. This has direct implications for our society.

First, it means that national attention needs to be paid to this particular area.

Second, it means that public monies need to be set aside for studying the problem.

Third, it means that significant changes may need to occur in some of the ways that our institutions currently operate.

As we push down the road toward developing research and prevention programs, perhaps in the future we will see professional fund raising activities devoted exclusively to solving the problem of child visitation interference.

I certainly hope so.

ABOUT THE AUTHOR

Dr. Turkat is an internationally known clinical psychologist, who has published over 75 books, book chapters and professional publications. He has served on the faculties of the Vanderbilt University School of Medicine, the University of North Carolina at Greensboro, and the University of Florida College of Medicine. For 15 years, Dr. Turkat served as the Associate Editor of the *Journal of Psychopathology and Behavioral Assessment*, a scientific periodical, which is received in 25 countries around the world.

You may contact Dr. Turkat as follows:

Address: Dr. Ira Daniel Turkat
            Drawer 1447
            Venice, Florida 34284

Telephone: (941) 488-8093

Facsimile: (941) 488-9407